Errol Bray, the Artistic Director of Interplay, is the author of *Playbuilding: a guide for group creation of plays with young people*  He co-founded Shopfront Theatre for Young People in Director there for nine years. Until 1993 he was the Director Victoria.

The International Festival of Young Playw ears in Australia. It was founded in 1984 by Errol Bray ar ice in Warragul, Victoria, and in 1994 in Townsville, Queer

The aims of the Interplay Festival are: to celebrate the creative richness of young playwrights; to provide an international meeting place where their work can be discussed, workshopped and performed; to provide an international forum for the ideas of young playwrights; and to offer the general public access to their work.

**4th Interplay Festival
Funding Support and Sponsors** (**in**'-ter *pla̰y*)

Major Benefactors

The Literature Board of the Australia Council
James Cook University of North Queensland
The Council of the City of Townsville
Arts Queensland
The British Council
The Aboriginal & Torres Strait Islander Arts Committee
 of the Australia Council

Sponsors

Advance Systems Technology Pty Ltd, Townsville
ATN Channel Seven, Sydney
Australian Youth Foundation
The Commonwealth Foundation, London
Currency Press, Sydney
Hermit Park Bus Service, Townsville
Philip Leong Investments Pty Ltd, Townsville
Students Union of James Cook University
Sunshine Television Network, Townsville
Switchboard Arts Consultancy, Sydney
Thai International Restaurant and the Townsville Thai community
Thrifty Rent-a-Car
The Townsville Bulletin

Supporters

Amcal Chemist, Flinders Mall
ASSITEJ International
Australian Film, Television & Radio School, Sydney
Canadian Consulate General, Sydney
Community Aid Abroad Shop, Townsville
German Consulate General, Sydney
Hardings Solicitors, Sydney
La Luna Youth Theatre, Townsville
McDonalds Family Restaurants
Malanda Milk
New Zealand High Commission, Canberra
Queensland Theatre Company
School of Education Students' Association, JCU
Shopfront Theatre for Young People, Sydney
Sydney Theatre Company
Townsville Civic Theatre
Townsville College of TAFE
Townsville Feminist Collective
Trade Winds Tea
Tropic Line Theatre Company, Townsville

Young Playwrights

Eleven New Plays

Edited by

ERROL BRAY

CURRENCY PRESS • SYDNEY

First published in 1994 by
Currency Press Pty Ltd,
PO Box 452 Paddington
NSW 2021, Australia

Copyright *Young Playwrights* 1994 © Errol Bray. Our smaller global village © *Errol Bray*, Three Out © *Rob Bartel*, Five Visits from Mr Whitcomb © *Carter L. Bays*, Skin © *Neil Biswas*, Styx and Bones © *Samantha Dickinson*, Windows © *Richard Hannay*, Market of Lives © *Le Quy Duong*, Journey to the West © *Lee Chee Keng*, Heart of the Land © *Darren Manns*, On the Island © *Pawel Marcin Nowak*, Ji-Da (The Bird) © *Amy Roberts*, Lovepuke © *Duncan Sarkies*

This book is copyright. Apart from any fair dealing for the purpose of private study, research or review, as permitted under the Copyright Act, no part may be reproduced by any process without written permission. Inquiries concerning publication, translation or recording rights should be addressed to Currency Press.

Any performance or public reading of any of these plays is forbidden unless a licence has been received from the author or the author's agent. The purchase of this book in no way gives the purchaser the right to perform the play in public, whether by means of a staged production or a reading. All applications for public performance should be addressed to Currency Press.

National Library of Australia
Cataloguing-in-Publication data

       Young playwrights

       ISBN 0 86819 415 8.

I. Drama - 20th century. Youths' writings. I. Bray, Errol.

808.8200835

Printed by Bridge Printery, Rosebery, NSW/Design and illustrations by Jana Hartig/Set by Currency, Sydney/Permission to quote from *Love is in the Air* kindly given by J. Albert & Sons.

Publication of this title was assisted by the Commonwealth Government through the Australia Council, its arts funding and advisory body.

Contents

Our smaller global village *Errol Bray*   vii

3 Out *Rob Bartel*   1
Five Visits from Mr Whitcomb *Carter L. Bays*   25
Skin *Neil Biswas*   50
Styx and Bones *Samantha Dickinson*   63
Windows *Richard Hannay*   94
Market of Lives *Le Quy Duong*   106
Journey to the West *Lee Chee Keng*   147
Heart of the Land *Darren Manns*   160
On the Island *Pawel Marcin Nowak*   167
Ji-Da (The Bird) *Amy Roberts*   175
Lovepuke *Duncan Sarkies*   188

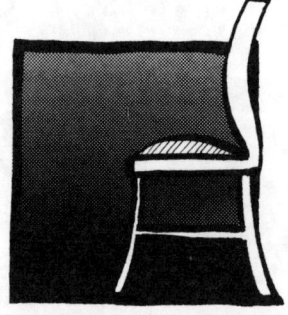

Our smaller global village

Errol Bray

These eleven plays have been selected from the work of the fifty-one young writers from twenty-four nations who were invited to be Delegates at the 4th International Festival of Young Playwrights in Townsville in July 1994. They were selected for their qualities of imagination and dramatic power and also because they are accessible on the page. They also have dramatic strengths that make them readily producible. It is not a 'best of' selection, as that would be almost impossible to achieve in such a strong field of plays and writers. But as a group of plays, this selection gives a good picture of the range of interests and styles the Interplay writers have, and of the raw talent of the new generation of playwrights in the world.

These plays range in style from the sophisticated word-play of Duncan Sarkie's *Lovepuke* to the epic power of Le Quy Duong's *Market of Lives* and, in another direction, to the deceptive simplicity of Pawel Nowak's *On The Island*. Perhaps there are no lines of direct influence, but it is tempting to point out the Chekhovian subtlety of a play like Neil Biswas' *Skin* and to go on and reveal young examples of Brecht, Miller and even Joe Orton. But these plays come at you with individual voices and individual points of view. Each play reveals the developing style of a new dramatist and the concerns and issues that are engaging young creative minds.

That sounds rather serious, but many of the plays use humour to make their points. Samantha Dickinson's *Styx and Bones* is broadly comic and purely for fun. However, it still reveals a way of thinking in the world that is a touch unsettling. Carter L. Bays uses humour in *Five Visits from Mr. Whitcomb* quite carefully and deliberately to achieve an unsettling effect. Like many other good comic writers, he makes you laugh but leaves you very worried about the state of the world.

Three of the plays have a similarity in the way they weave traditional myths into stories on contemporary issues. The plays by two young Aboriginal writers - Amy Roberts' *Ji-da (The Bird)* and Darren Manns' *Heart of the Land* - are almost morality tales in the way they use Aboriginal myths and dreamings to encourage change in the lives of their characters. In very similar fashion, Lee Chee Keng uses a traditional Chinese myth in his *Journey to the West* to counterpoint his contemporary generation-gap story. It is probably true that only in Singapore, where the implications of the myth could be fully grasped, could Lee's play have its full impact. This is another aspect of this collection that is notable. Many of the plays are strongly rooted in their specific cultures and yet they still speak universally. Perhaps this is a reflection of our smaller global village where all countries' concerns are the world's concerns. But I think these writers also have the ability to tap issues at their core and bring us the passion of youth along with the emerging skills of good writers. Although *Windows* by Richard Hannay is a cry of protest about a particular injustice in Australia, it has intense relevance for most countries. The family relationships at the heart of Rob Bartel's *3 Out* speak sadly and intensely to Western societies in particular, but have wide implications universally. *Lovepuke* is a New Zealand play but it could sit happily in a theatre season in any Western country. It seems to tap directly into the relationship concerns of contemporary young adults everywhere, with funny and intense revelations.

To fit a range of plays into one book we have of necessity chosen a number of short plays, but each one seems to me to be the right length for its subject. *Skin* is quite brief but it is a beautifully polished gem of exactly the right size for what Neil wants to say. *Market of Lives* is a larger play and its epic story requires time and expansiveness. In many ways we see here writers who are not yet compelled by commercial pressures to write to a standard length for a standard cast size. They are writing plays only to meet the dramatic needs of their stories and their ideas. The refreshing results are enough justification for ignoring theatre tradition.

Today, we seem to know so much about the world through television but we still need writers and dramatists to unveil the heart and soul of national identities and issues. We know the facts from television but we need more. We need to understand emotions and reasons. Writers do that for us. These young writers are doing it already and with passion and insight. If we could publish all the plays from the 4th Interplay a rich resource of enormous talent and commitment would be revealed. These eleven plays have a difficult task in representing all young writers in the world. I think they do it remarkably well in this collection of exciting, thoughtful and skilful dramas.

Townsville, June 1994

3 Out

ROB BARTEL

Rob Bartel was born in 1976 in Canada but spent three years of his childhood in Jamaica. He lives in Saskatchewan and last year had a play performed in the Fringe Theatre Festival in Saskatoon.

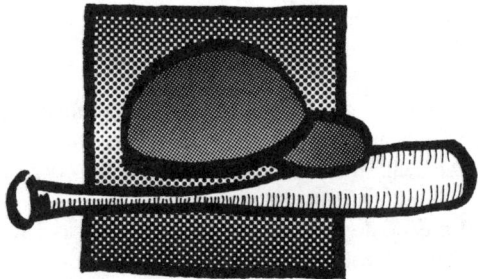

CHARACTERS

TV VOICE 1
TV VOICE 2
LYNN
TY
LISA
JIMMY

Scene One

The Clarke living room. A baseball jersey hangs on the wall, enclosed behind a pane of glass. Ty is watching a videotape of an old ball game. It's a Sunday afternoon. He's alone.)

TV VOICE 1 Well, we're back, folks. Top of the ninth; Jays up by three.

TV VOICE 2 That's right, John. It's been an easy game for Toronto, so far today. Things were looking like rain there for a while, but it cleared up.

TV VOICE 1 Well, Kismett's up to bat for the Phillies. They've got two outs and the potential to score with Chouse on third. Let's see how Kismett does. Here's the pitch.

TV VOICE 2 Nice clean hit. Headed for just a little bit left of center. Looks like this one's going to land in the hole, John.

TV VOICE 1 No, Clarke comes up with it! If I didn't know any better, I would have sworn that Kismett had himself an easy double there. Could have put themselves on the board with that one. Incredible diving catch by Terry Clarke.

TV VOICE 2 Yup, the Blue Jays found a fine left fielder in Terry Clarke. I don't know where they'd be without him.-

Ty presses rewind briefly.

TV VOICE 2 --I don't know where they'd be without him.

Ty rewinds again.

TV VOICE 2 --where they'd be without him.

Ty rewinds again as Lynn enters, returning from work.

	LYNN	Hi, Ty. Jimmy home? [*She exits to the bedroom to change.*]
	TY	He's practising over at Zilch's. [*He releases the rewind button.*]
	TV VOICE 2	--It's been an easy game for Toronto, so far today. Things were looking like rain... [*The tape continues quietly.*]
	LYNN	What are you watching?
	TY	Nothing. How was work?
	LYNN	Don't ask. You and Jimmy forget to go help Mrs. Lendon?

She goes out.

	TY	Not really.
	LYNN	[*She re-enters.*] Not really. Jeez, Ty, if you're going to lie to me, at least do a better job than that, okay? All she wanted was a few kids to help her put in her garden.
	TV VOICE 1	...No, Clarke comes up with it! If I didn't know any better...
	LYNN	What the hell are you watching, Ty?
	TY	Just one of Dad's games.
	TV VOICE 2	...Terry Clarke. I don't know where they'd be...
	LYNN	[*Grabbing the remote control and stopping the VCR. She moves to the TV, turns it off, then ejects the tape from the VCR.*] Damn it, Ty, where did you get this?
	TY	The basement.
	LYNN	I'm too tired to argue now, okay, Ty? Here, take the tape and put it away, somewhere. We'll talk about it later.
	TY	When do you want me to wake you up?
	LYNN	At five, or so. Then we can cook some soup or something for supper before I go back to work again, alright?

TY	Yeah, okay.
LYNN	And if Jimmy comes home and wants to play his guitar, tell him he'd better do it quietly, okay?
TY	Yeah.
LYNN	Were there any calls?
TY	Yeah. Mister Johnson wants the rent.
LYNN	Shit. He told me we had until Wednesday. I'll call him back later. Anything else?
TY	That guy from Ontario called again. He said he had some forms for you to sign or something.
LYNN	I'd like to see them come ask that to my face. Damn privately funded jackasses! Did you hang up on him like I told you?
TY	Yeah. I'm gonna go out and play catch with Lisa, okay?
LYNN	Getting ready to try out tomorrow?
TY	Yeah.
LYNN	Alright. Go ahead, then. Just be back to wake me up at five, okay?

Scene Two

Ty and Lisa play catch outside.

LISA	You want a pop fly?
TY	No. I know how to catch those.
LISA	Everyone knows how to catch them. I'm asking if you want to catch one.
TY	Then the answer is still no, okay?
LISA	Someone's sure grouchy today. Has Jimmy been acting like an ass again?

TY   Jimmy's not an ass.

LISA   No, he just acts like one a lot of the time.

TY   Give him a little credit, Lisa.

LISA   Yeah, right... How come you weren't helping Mrs. Lendon plant this morning?

TY   I don't know. Jimmy didn't want to go.

LISA   You could have gone by yourself.

TY   It isn't as if you bothered to tell me you'd be there.

LISA   Well, just because you didn't show, Dad made me look after my little sister and all her bratty little friends.

TY   You used to be just as bratty, remember, so don't get too up in arms about it.

LISA   At least I was cute back then.

TY   I don't know what kind of kid I was. We don't have any photos or anything from before we came here.

LISA   You were an ugly baby. It shows in your eyes.

TY   You didn't even know me until I was in kindergarten.

LISA   I said it shows in your eyes, didn't I?

TY   Right.

LISA   Remember when I got a bunch of us Grade Ones to beat you up at recess?

TY   That was some other kid, not me.

LISA   Was it?

TY   You probably got so excited you forgot who you were after. You're like that sometimes.

LISA   I am not.

TY   Yes you are. You still get all stressed out at ball games, at least.

LISA   So ball gets me pumped. Big deal.

TY   Yeah, just don't go around swinging from vines and beating your chest in the outfield, there, okay?

LISA   What chest?

TY   Oh, shut up. You know what I mean.

LISA   You're just jealous.

TY   About what?

LISA   That I'm a year older than you and that much more mature.

TY   You? Mature?

LISA   Yes, do you have a problem with that?

TY   Well, I may be a year younger but you're just plain weird.

LISA   So, are you gonna come pick me up so we can go try out tomorrow?

TY   Are you kidding? I'm going to get there before you and take your jersey number.

LISA   Yeah, you take my number and I'll beat the crap out of you. You're picking me up at 6:45, tomorrow, and we're walking to try-outs together, whether you like it or not.

TY   I'm not going to pick you up.

LISA   Yes you are. Why? Because you're a schmuck. A schmuck who happens to be my best friend, mind you, but still a schmuck. Now throw the ball.

TY   Yeah, alright. But if I roll my ankle, or something, crossing good old Gopher Park, there, though, I'm blaming you.

LISA   I'll kiss it better, okay, just throw the dumb ball.

Scene Three

Evening. Jimmy sits on the porch, playing guitar. An opened case of beer lies on the floor beside him. Ty enters with the ball and glove.

JIMMY   Hey, Sport.

TY   Hey. How did practice go?

JIMMY   Ah, Zilch was being a wench, again. She just goofed off and wouldn't play anything real.

TY   You guys should kick her out the band, then.

JIMMY   Yeah. Right, Ty. It doesn't work that way, alright?

TY   It's not as if you can't find another violinist. Besides, I think it sounds dumb.

JIMMY   You're the one that sounds dumb. Anyways, it's more than that. She's just so damn random, that's all. I mean, if she's in the wrong mood, she'll deliberately play everything in the wrong key, or something, just to piss the rest of us off.

TY   Wenching out.

JIMMY   Yeah, but she's not doing it to be a bitch, though. She just finds it funny.

TY   Yeah. Did you guys come up with any new riffs or anything?

JIMMY   Nah. More or less just hashed over the same old stuff. I'm so tired of that shit, Ty. Tired of Zilch, tired of the guys, tired of everything .

TY   But you guys sound good.

JIMMY   Shut up, alright Ty? I'm not in the mood for your crap tonight.

TY   Yeah. You want something to eat?

JIMMY   Sure. Go crawl into the furnace and give me a call when you're well-done. Shit, Ty, just leave me alone, okay?

TY   Lisa called you an asshole, today. I stuck up for you, too.

JIMMY   Bravo. Do you want a damn medallion?

TY		You are an asshole, though. Lisa knows it, I know it, you know it.
JIMMY		Yes, everybody knows that Jimmy T. Clarke is an asshole. And when that asshole isn't holding a guitar, he's holding a book, and when he isn't holding a book, he's holding a bottle. Music, fine literature, and cheap alcohol, Ty. Those three things can separate men from apes, but they sure as hell don't keep us assholes apart.
TY		How come you're like this, Jimmy?
JIMMY		How come? Some things are just in our nature, Ty.
TY		You're full of shit.
JIMMY		Well, you eat what mother luck puts before you. From the voice of experience, Sport: when you're finding your way around the city of life, don't hang a left at the intersection of First and Love.
TY		Love...? The only girl you ever dated was Zilch and she doesn't count.
JIMMY		You and your damn grade-school mentality, Ty. All you've ever known are a bunch of seventh grade whores.
TY		I don't see why you and Zilch ever broke up. I mean, you're perfect for each other: you're both assholes.
JIMMY		Yeah.
TY		'Yeah'. What's that supposed to mean?
JIMMY		It means 'Yeah, some things don't work out, no matter how much you try.' Two rules to live by, Ty: First, never go out with a tomboy. Second, never go out with your best friend.
TY		Like me and Lisa, eh?
JIMMY		Like you and Lisa.
TY		You're full of shit.
JIMMY		Wish I was, Ty. Wish I was full of shit, wish I had never gone out with Zilch, wish Mom didn't have to pull two jobs just to support a couple of bums like us, wish a lot of things... Wish I was full of shit, Ty. Maybe then I'd be able to take a bit more of it.

TY	What do you really wish for, Jimmy?
JIMMY	You still like baseball?
TY	Yeah... Yeah, of course. Like father, like son, right?
JIMMY	Well, I wish you didn't like baseball. I wish you hated it, in fact. But... But I wish a lot of things, don't I?
TY	It's because of him, isn't it.
JIMMY	'Him'... I just don't like drawing comparisons, okay?
TY	Comparisons of what?
JIMMY	Let's just shut up about it, okay Ty?
TY	You're drunk!
JIMMY	Yeah, but at least I'm truthful about it. Get me another one, could you, Sport? I've got a headache.
TY	Yeah, okay... Can I have a sip?
JIMMY	Wouldn't Mom just love me then, eh? Make her darling child grow up just like me.
TY	Just a little bit. It's not like I haven't had any before.
JIMMY	Yeah, well, it wasn't on my hands then and it isn't going to be, now.
TY	You're so damn full of yourself, you know that? A damn drunkard, sitting there, scared of what Mom might do.
JIMMY	You want a sip? Here, have a bottle, take the rest of the case. Just don't go putting any blame on me, you little shit. [*TY opens one and sips a bit.*] Damn empty victory, isn't it, Sport?
TY	Shut up.
JIMMY	You think I chose to be like this, Ty? It's called fate and I don't have bloody much to do with it, okay? That's why I'm a fucking drunk, that's why you're gonna end up just like me: playing guitar in a band that no one will ever hear

and messing around with your best friend.

TY: I'm not doing anything with Lisa!

JIMMY: That's why... That's... That's why everything!

TY: Everything what?

JIMMY: Everything nothing. Just leave me alone, okay?

TY: I never knew him, Jimmy.

JIMMY: Just as well. He was a shit.

TY: He was not! He was one of the greatest ball players Canada ever produced. He had blond hair, brown eyes, was 6'3", threw righthanded, but batted left. They called him 'Mr. Nice.'

JIMMY: The books don't know anything, Ty, and neither do you.

TY: Maybe because you never bothered to tell me anything, Jimmy. He was my dad, too!

JIMMY: Funny. He sure wasn't mine. Didn't act like it, anyways.

TY: Don't say that.

JIMMY: Do you know how he died? I bet your books never told you that eh?

TY: He got sick.

JIMMY: Yeah, he got sick. Stopped eating. He said it was something with his throat or stomach or something but when the doctors ran the tests, they couldn't find anyting. They put him on intravenous. You know, did what they could, but in the end, he just died. Just like a dog or a goldfish or a budgie or a... or... or anything. He just died, Ty. That's all.

TY: Why?

JIMMY: Look, Sport, I really don't want to talk about this... Let's get something to eat, okay?

TY: No. I'm not really all that hungry.

3 Out

JIMMY You never made it home for supper. Didn't wake Mom up, either. She kind of wanted me to emphasize that to you.

TY Yeah, I know. I just didn't feel like coming home. She was in a bad mood.

JIMMY Yeah.

TY She didn't say anything, did she?

JIMMY To me? You know how she is.

TY She caught me watching one of Dad's games. I found it in your closet.

JIMMY So you're the rat who's been poking around in there, eh? If you're looking for dirty magazines or something, don't bother.

TY No... I was looking for that scrapbook you had about him.

JIMMY You remember that?

TY Kind of. There was that one magazine picture of Mom and Dad in our old house, right?

JIMMY Yeah... Yeah... Well, don't bother looking anymore. I burnt that when you were ten or so.

TY How come Mom won't let us watch his old games.

JIMMY Ah, it's just the way she is.

TY She wasn't really mad, was she?

JIMMY Kind of. She didn't say anything about that, though.

TY Yeah, that guy from Ontario called again, too.

JIMMY Don't worry about it. It's his job, that's all.

TY Well, he doesn't have to be such a jerk about it.

JIMMY No, but he's just a corporate puppet, you know? A political junkie, so there's nothing we can do. Here, give me that bottle and go to bed. You're not drinking it.

	TY	Shut up, I'll finish it.
	JIMMY	Yeah, well, I'm going to bed, then. Don't get yourself too pissed. [*He goes.*]

Scene Four

Inside the Clarke home on the following morning. Lynn is eating breakfast when Jimmy walks in.

	LYNN	You're up early. Got a job or something?
	JIMMY	No. I just figured that I probably think better in the morning.
	LYNN	Well, it doesn't show much but, sure, I'll buy it. What are you thinking about?
	JIMMY	I don't know. Just some things Ty said.
	LYNN	Lisa didn't hit him with a baseball bat again, did she?
	JIMMY	No. Nothing like that.
	LYNN	Good, because I'd rather not have to talk to that girl's mother again. The lady's a shark.
	JIMMY	Like father, like son.
	LYNN	Or mother and daughter, as the case is.
	JIMMY	Yeah.
	LYNN	What kind of things was Ty saying?
	JIMMY	I don't know. I probably did most of the talking.
	LYNN	Now, why does that not surprise me?
	JIMMY	It should. You and I never really talk.
	LYNN	Well, we're doing it right now, aren't we?
	JIMMY	That's just because I got up early.
	LYNN	Maybe I'm hinting at something, here.

JIMMY Like what?

LYNN Like get up early every morning, you big lout.

JIMMY I can't do that, Mom. You're always so full of energy and stuff. I can't work that way.

LYNN You never tried, that's what your problem is. I mean, have you ever watched Ty play ball? He stole more bases last year than anyone on the team. Even Lisa. Sometimes, you've just got to lead off a bit and take some risks, Jimmy.

JIMMY That's not what's different between Ty and me, Mom.

LYNN No?

JIMMY No. I mean... I mean, I just wish he read more books.

LYNN How come?

JIMMY It would just make things a whole lot easier to explain, that's all.

LYNN Ty's not dumb, Jimmy. Heck, you're the one who failed twice, not him.

JIMMY Yeah, but that was because of social problems, not because I was dumb.

LYNN Social problems, my arse, Jimmy. You never paid any attention in class, that's what your problem was. Just sat in the back row and farted around the whole time.

JIMMY I happen to come from a dysfunctional family, alright?

LYNN This family isn't dysfunctional, Jimmy. You are. Now go wake up your brother or he's going to miss the school bus again.

JIMMY He's sick. I checked on him, already.

LYNN Don't be such a lazy ass.

JIMMY What? I checked on him, I said.

Lynn goes.

JIMMY It's a dysfunctional family, Mother.

Lynn returns, marching Ty in front of her. He is hungover.

LYNN He's looking more and more like you all the time, Jimmy. Ty, go wash up. You're going to school anyways.

TY It had nothing to do with him, Mom.

JIMMY Hey, Sport. Don't try and cover up for Big Brother, now, okay?

TY This is my fault, though.

LYNN Ty. Shower. Now.

JIMMY Listen to your mother, Ty.

TY But, this ... you're both crazy.

He goes, pounding once on the doorframe as he leaves.

JIMMY It just happened, Mom. He'll be okay.

LYNN I know he'll be okay! What the hell did you think you were doing, getting him drunk.

JIMMY I wasn't really thinking straight.

LYNN You weren't thinking straight. You're never thinking straight, Jimmy! I can't live like this anymore. I can't be your damned Peter Pan and Wendy anymore. Maybe I could when I was younger, Jimmy, but I can't now. I'm too old. Inside I'm too old. It's... It's like giving birth to you again and again and again... Everyday I see you.

JIMMY Ty's a good kid, Mom. He'll be alright.

LYNN I'm not going to let him turn out like you, Jimmy! I can't take another you!

JIMMY You've lived through two of us, already. What's a third, Mom?

LYNN Get out, Jimmy. Don't say anything, just get out. [*Jimmy doesn't move.*] Why do you have to do this to me, Jimmy?

JIMMY It's in my nature.

3 Out

LYNN In your nature. When's it gonna stop? When are you going to realize that you can't be a kid forever?

JIMMY I wish I could have been a kid, Mom! I never was! You and Dad never gave me the chance.

LYNN You never took the chance! You holed yourself up reading books all day, or playing that stupid guitar of yours, or going over to snort a line at Zilch's house!

JIMMY I don't do that stuff anymore. Neither does Zilch.

LYNN Well, maybe you guys should start again. Go out with a bang, Jimmy. Die with a fucking needle in your vein, I don't care. Just don't come to me saying that your Dad and I wouldn't let you play ball or we didn't buy you the right toys as a kid or any of this shit, okay? You never took the chance to be a kid and, as long as you're in this house, you're keeping Ty from being one, too.

JIMMY It's not me that's kept either of us from being kids, Mom. It's because you married a damn ball player and let him be the only kid in the family.

LYNN You have no idea what's going on, do you. I can work my ass off for you and Ty and you'll just throw it all away. Every time. You're twenty-one years old, Jimmy. Please, if you're going to stay, something's got to change.

JIMMY No, I... I packed up last night, already. I'll just get the guitar and go, alright? [*He kisses her forehead.*]

LYNN Yeah. Yeah, alright...

Jimmy goes to his room.

LYNN [*to herself.*] Anything's alright...

TY [*entering, hair wet from shower.*] Am I really going to school? My head's doing some really funny stuff to me right now.

LYNN Stay home, I guess. The bus went by, already, and I don't have time to drive you. Are you hungry for anything?

TY No. I just threw up. I'm going to bed, okay?

JIMMY [*passing through with suitcase and guitar case.*] Take care of your mother, alright Sport? These things just happen.

He goes.

TY You made him leave, didn't you.

LYNN Yeah. He has to learn sometime, Ty.

TY I'm the one who got drunk... He tried to stop me, Mom.

LYNN I know... I know, Ty.

TY You know? Well, if you know, don't kick him out!

LYNN I... I have to, Ty... That's just the way things work, okay?

TY Where's he gonna stay?

LYNN He'll find something, Ty. Please... just

TY You can't do this to him, Mom!

LYNN He's doing it to himself, Ty.

TY But you can't.

LYNN Please, Ty... You're just going to make your headache worse. It... It doesn't matter anymore. It's too late for that... Really...

TY Jimmy's not like that, Mom.

LYNN Go to bed, Ty. I'll be at work when you wake up.

Scene Five

In the living room, that afternoon. TY is watching the ball video again.

TV VOICE 2 Nice clean hit. Headed for just a little bit left of center. Looks like this one's going to land in the hole, John.

TV VOICE 1 No, Clarke comes up with it! If I didn't know any better, I would have sworn that Kismett had himself an easy double there. Could have put themselves on the board with that one. Incredible diving catch by Terry Clarke.

TV VOICE 2	Yup, the Blue Jays found a fine left fielder in Terry Clarke. I don't know where they'd be without him.
TV VOICE 1	Probably at the bottom of the league, unfortunately. The Jays haven't been doing too hot these past couple seasons.
TV VOICE 2	Yes, it's surprising that Clarke's stats are as good as they are. Playing for the wrong team can sure bring a good fielder like him down, John. That's why I always get a little nervous when they start talking trades.
TV VOICE 1	Well, while the teams are switching off, why don't you let us in on the latest word from the Cleveland trades.

TY turns it off with the remote and sits silently for a while.

TY	They should have traded you, Dad. They could have got all the money they ever wanted out of you then, couldn't they? You know what? If they would've done that, then they wouldn't have to send that guy from Ontario after us, now. Hell, I don't even know what he wants, Dad. It's about you and I guess that's all that matters, right? Everything's about you. Everything. Just because I'm your kid, I've got to play ball, I've got to be a fielder, I've got to steal bases just like you. I'm scared of the ball, Dad. I'm scared of the ball and no one believes me. Why am I even talking to you. Hell, it's not like I remember you or anything. I'm not your son. I don't have any idea who you are, except what I read in the damned encyclopedia. You threw right-handed, batted left. Every single one of them mentions that and I had no idea until Lisa first showed me your ball card! I hate her, I hate you, I hate Jimmy, I hate everything... I hate... I hate baseball. All these years I've played fucking baseball and I played it for you! You were the highest-paid ball player of your time, too. Where's that money now, huh? Where's the money now? You gave it all to the fucking charities and to the league and to the Jays and to the mayor and to the orphanage and to everybody but us! Baseball's greatest family, and look at us now! Jimmy left a note saying that he's gonna room with Zilch. I hope they tear each other's throats out or something. Probably will, too, that's what's stupid. Did you ever fall in love, Dad? With Mom or someone else? Anyone at all? It was always just you and baseball, wasn't it. That's how Jimmy and Zilch are, too. Jimmy likes her so much that he'll do anything for her. Even if it means blowing himself up. I mean, if she wanted him to stop playing guitar, he'd do it for her. She'd ask that, too. She knows it would kill him, but she'd be crazy enough to ask. He wouldn't do it out of love or whatever, either. He'd just do it because they're old friends. It's a guilt thing. You and baseball were just like that, weren't you. Baseball wanted a 6'3" Mr. Nice so you blew yourself up to do it. Blew all of us up. And the whole time, you knew exactly what you were doing, too. You knew everything and you still did it. You didn't

have a choice, I guess. Jimmy didn't either, I bet. I don't know. Maybe you're both full of shit, I don't know. Are you like Jimmy? He sees things in straight lines. I mean everything's so clear and definite to him. I'm not like that. I try, but I'm not. That's the dumbest thing about him, Dad. He'll always have some really stupid ideas and stuff, but, when it's all over, he's still batting a thousand. Gets it right, every time. I do things with the greatest intentions. I just don't do them right.

Scene Six

Ty has gone to meet Lisa at the school bus dropoff. They're on their way home.

LISA   You're playing sick so you don't have to walk me to try-outs today, right?

TY   Stop bugging me. I said I'd pick you up and I will, okay?

LISA   You better, because I know people who'd bust your kneecaps for a buck.

TY   I'm accident-prone enough, okay?

LISA   That's for sure. Why weren't you at school, then, if you weren't skipping.

TY   I told you, I was sick.

LISA   Well, you're not sick anymore. What have you got, anyways, morning sickness?

TY   No, I'm just sick, okay?

LISA   That was a joke, Ty. You were supposed to laugh, not answer.

TY   Yeah, yeah. I'm still feeling a little queasy, that's all.

LISA   Then why did you come to meet me?

TY   I don't know. I just felt like seeing you, having you around, you know?

LISA   You're a very sweet boy, Ty. When you're not being a schmuck, that is.

TY   I'm not being a schmuck now, am I?

	LISA	No. A little weird, maybe, but not a schmuck. Why, what's the matter?
	TY	Nothing's the matter. Everything's perfectly fine, okay?
	LISA	Grouchy as heck, but sure, we can call it perfectly fine if you want.
	TY	Jimmy got kicked out this morning.
	LISA	About time.
	TY	Why do you hate him so much?
	LISA	Well, can you see living with your mom for your whole life? It would drive me nuts, I know that.
	TY	But he didn't do anything.
	LISA	Well, if he got kicked out, then he obviously must have done something .
	TY	He didn't. I got... It was me, okay? I goofed up and he got kicked out.
	LISA	You goof up a lot, though. Remember when you fell out of the tree and broke your arm in Grade Six. Right before ball season, too.
	TY	Yeah... I slipped.
	LISA	Yeah, well, that's what I call goofing up, and I don't see how something like that is gonna get Jimmy kicked out.
	TY	I got drunk, alright? I stayed up last night, talking with Jimmy, and, after he went to bed, I had a few bottles. He had nothing to do with it.
	LISA	A few bottles. What's a few?
	TY	I don't know. I wasn't exactly in any kind of state to keep track.
	LISA	So your mom found you passed out on the porch in the morning?
	TY	No. I guess Jimmy must have brought me in or something. Hell, Lisa, I don't know. I feel like I don't know anything anymore.
	LISA	Where did he go?

TY   Zilch's. Where else?

LISA   I thought they broke up.

TY   Yeah. Doesn't make any difference, though, does it?

LISA   Sure it does. He needs a place to stay and she's not going to let him stay if they still hate each other.

TY   They hated each other while they were still going out and she let him stay for weekends and stuff.

LISA   Yeah, maybe. I wouldn't put up with your crap if I hated you, though.

TY   I'd put up with yours.

LISA   Yeah, but that just goes to show how much dumber you are.

TY   It's not dumb. You and I are really good friends, that's all.

LISA   But if you and I hated each other, then we obviously couldn't be really good friends, could we?

TY   Remember when you went out with Jay?

LISA   Yes, unfortunately. He kissed like a fish.

TY   Well, I hated you for a whole week. You and him both.

LISA   You shouldn't have. He and I only went out for two nights and I faked sick for the second.

TY   Yeah, but...

LISA   You were jealous, that's all.

TY   Yeah, so? I thought you were really dumb for going out with a schmuck like him, that's all.

LISA   You're the schmuck, remember. Jay was just a jerk.

TY   Lisa?

LISA Yes, Your Schmuckness?

TY I'm not a jerk, am I?

LISA No. I mean, you can be sometimes, and, for all I know, you may kiss like a fish, but you're usually pretty bearable, yup.

TY What if I gave you a present?

LISA I'd take it and run, why?

TY Close your eyes.

LISA What, are you getting revenge for that bat incident? Your mom already made me apologize for that.

TY Just close your damn eyes. I don't have to do this.

LISA Yeah, alright. Do anything funny, though, and I'll punch your lights out.

She closes her eyes and Ty tries to kiss her. She pushes him away and he falls down.

[*Wiping her mouth*] What, are you going to tell me you love me or something, too? You're so full of shit, Ty. You've been around Jimmy too much.

TY Yeah, well, we're all full of shit, Lisa! Take a look sometime!

He runs off.

LISA Ty! Come back, I didn't mean it that way. Ty!

Scene Seven

Zilch's house. Jimmy is lounging comfortably and holding a beer bottle. Ty stands.

JIMMY Hey, Sport.

TY Where's Zilch?

JIMMY She went out to buy some more groceries. It looks like I'll be staying for a while. Do you want to stick around for supper? She's cooking up some scrambled eggs.

TY   No.

JIMMY   No? I thought you like scrambled eggs.

TY   How come you're doing this, Jimmy?

JIMMY   Doing what? We're not still talking about eggs, here, are we?

TY   You were the one talking about eggs.

JIMMY   How come I'm doing what, then?

TY   [*He gestures about the room.*] All of this! I mean, I thought you and Zilch were over.

JIMMY   We were. These things change, Sport. What's the big deal?

TY   Nothing, it's just that... It's just that you said going out with Zilch was a mistake.

JIMMY   Yeah, so?

TY   How can you do this again? You're never going to be able to please her, Jimmy! You're never going to be good enough for her.

JIMMY   You don't think I know that, Sport?

TY   Then why the hell are you and her going out again?

JIMMY   These little mistakes are in my nature, Ty. I've told you that before.

TY   They're not! There's nothing in your nature! Nothing! Just like there's nothing in mine, either! I kissed Lisa today and she laughed in my face!

JIMMY   Why did you do that, Sport?

TY   Because of you. You made me think I had to. Like it wasn't my choice or something. Just like Dad didn't have any choice playing ball and you didn't have any choice but to ruin what you had with Zilch. I'm just trying to do something right, for once. I try to do something right, here, and you keep changing your story on me.

JIMMY	My story hasn't changed, Ty. Do you think I can fix things up between Zilch and I, here? We'll never do that. She and I are just gonna have to learn to put up with each other's shit and move on. We both know we're stuck, Sport. We can't change. It's too late for that. Besides, some things don't work out, no matter how hard you try, right?	
TY	Dad made the choice to play ball and it killed him and it looks like it killed you, as well. Hell, maybe it's killed Mom and I, too, I don't know, but at least she and I aren't going to sell out like you two have.	
JIMMY	Go home, Sport. Mom's not going to be happy if you miss two suppers in a row.	
TY	You keep thinking you and Dad are so different, don't you, Jimmy. You aren't! You aren't different at all!	
JIMMY	You never knew him, Ty.	
TY	I know. I know. I didn't know him.	
JIMMY	Go home.	

Scene Eight

The Clarke living room. The jersey is missing from its case and the glass is broken. Lynn is sitting on the floor, leaning against the wall, as Ty enters. Her hand is wrapped in gauze and she holds a cheque.

LYNN	Hey, Sport. You hungry?
TY	Yeah, sure.
LYNN	There are some leftover scrambled eggs in the fridge, okay?
TY	Sure, that'll be fine, I guess.
LYNN	Lisa called. Said you're still supposed to pick her up.
TY	I'm not trying out this year.
LYNN	Yeah.

TY	Are you alright, Mom?
LYNN	Yeah... I'm fine. That man from Ontario was here.
TY	Did you tell him off?
LYNN	I sold him Dad's jersey, Sport. The videotape, too.

She slowly tears the cheque to pieces.

THE END

Five Visits from Mr. Whitcomb

CARTER L. BAYS

Carter L. Bays was born in Cleveland in the United States in 1975. He has had four productions at his high school and in local theatres. *Five Visits from Mr Whitcomb* was produced off Broadway in 1993 and was the winning entry in the U.S. National Young Playwrights' Festival.

CHARACTERS

TOM, *a young man*
MR. WHITCOMB, *a tax auditor*
DR. BENTON, *a psychologist*
SHERIFF, *a sheriff*
FEDERAL AGENT, *a federal agent*
RON, *a goldfish*

SETTING

The eighties. A small cabin in the depths of a pine forest, somewhere in America.

Visit No. 1

Lights come up. We are in a cabin deep in the woods of America. The cabin is sparsely furnished: a bed, a table, a window, a door and a goldfish bowl on the table. In the bowl is Ron, a fish. Standing at the window, looking out in silent rapture, is Tom.

TOM What?... [*He turns to Ron, as if Ron had just said something.*] Yeah. [*He continues looking out the window, then turns back again.*] What? Yeah, I suppose you're right. [*He leaves his post at the window, and goes over to the table, on which is a pad of paper and a pencil. He sits down and starts writing.*] Okay... 'Things to do today: Number one, weed the garden. Number two, eat. Number three, feed the fish. [*A knock is heard at the door, three raps in perfect succession. Tom looks up, puzzled. Shrugging it off, he continues writing.*] Number four, hunt for rabbits. Number five, eat. [*Three more knocks are heard identical to the first three. Again, Tom looks up, but once more ignores it. He keeps writing.*] Number six, feed the fish. Number seven - [*Three more knocks, this time a little bit slower, more irritated.*] What's that noise, Ron?... Me neither.

Suddenly, through the window ducks the head of Mr. Whitcomb, a tax auditor.

WHITCOMB Excuse me... Excuse me... [*checking his papers*] Mr. Thomas Doe?

TOM Hello.

WHITCOMB Are you Mr. Thomas Doe?

Five Visits from Mr Whitcomb

TOM   I'm Tom, this is Ron. Who is it you're looking for?

WHITCOMB   May I come in please, Mr. Doe?

TOM   Who's Mr. Doe?

WHITCOMB   You are.

TOM   I'm Tom.

WHITCOMB   Fine. Can I come in please, Tom?

TOM   Sure.

He opens the door for Whitcomb, who enters.

WHITCOMB   Didn't you hear me knocking?

TOM   That was you?

WHITCOMB   Yes.

TOM   Oh. That explains it.

WHITCOMB   That explains what?

TOM   That sound. I was wondering where that sound was coming from. I thought maybe it was an animal, or a bird, or--

WHITCOMB   That's no concern of mine, Mr. Doe. I'm here on government business.

TOM   Oh.

WHITCOMB   My name is Whitcomb. I'm from the IRS. [*He waits for a reaction, gets none.*] I'm from the IRS. Internal Revenue Service.

TOM   Oh.

WHITCOMB   You don't seem surprised... Is something wrong, Mr. Doe?

TOM   No... I don't think so...

WHITCOMB   Well, when most people get a visit from the IRS, they tend to... You have heard of the IRS, haven't you?

TOM   Is, uh... Is that near Beanville?

WHITCOMB   Beanville? Mr. Doe, I'm a tax auditor. You know, Federal Income Tax?

TOM   Sorry, I've never heard of it.

WHITCOMB   Never heard of it?

TOM   I'm real sorry, Mr. Whitcomb.

WHITCOMB   No, no, don't apologise. It's quite alright... okay, look... Would you like me to explain the Internal Revenue Code?

TOM   Sure.

WHITCOMB   Are you in a hurry?

TOM   Well, actually, I do have to weed the garden, then eat, then feed the fish, then

WHITCOMB   I'll make it quick then. You see, Mr. Doe, the government

TOM   Tom.

WHITCOMB   Hm? Oh, sorry... The government, Tom... The government... is a business. And like any business, the government has certain jobs it must perform, like... fighting crime, and building roads, and fortifying our nuclear arsenal. And in order to do these jobs, the government needs something. And what do you think that is, Tom? What does the government need? [*Tom gives him a vacant look*] No idea? [*Another vacant look*] Money, Tom. Moolah. Good old dollars and cents. Anyway, the way the government makes this money is really quite simple: we just take a small percentage of each citizen's yearly income, in relation to such factors as the size of the salary, public philanthropy, real estate mortgages, and the cost of supporting any dependants. Are you following so far?

TOM   [*not following*] Yeah.

WHITCOMB   [*relieved*] Good... So, you understand the problem?

TOM   The problem?

Five Visits from Mr Whitcomb

WHITCOMB   Tom, you haven't paid your income tax in... [*he checks his sheet*] In... [*he turns the sheet over, and looks on the back*] Tom, you haven't paid your income tax!

TOM   And... that's bad?

WHITCOMB   Bad? BAD??? Of course it's bad, Tom! If nobody paid income tax, our government would go bankrupt! There would be widespread panic! Chaos in the street! We wouldn't be able to fortify our nuclear arsenal! We'd be overthrown by communists! Atheists! Anarchists! American civilization as we know it would crumble into oblivion! That's pretty bad, now wouldn't you say?

TOM   Yeah... and it's my fault?

WHITCOMB   Yes!...In a way... it would be... if it ever did happen, that is. But you see, Tom, we live in a democracy. And in a democracy we agree to live by the rules we lay out for ourselves, as a people. By following these rules, we all manage to live together happily. Jefferson called it the 'social contract'.

TOM   Lock.

WHITCOMB   What?

TOM   Lock.

WHITCOMB   Lock what?

TOM   John.

WHITCOMB   Lock John?

TOM   John Locke. John Locke came up with the social contract. Not Jefferson.

WHITCOMB   What?

TOM   Have you met my fish? Mr. Whitcomb, this is Ron. Ron, this is Mr. Whitcomb.

WHITCOMB   Wait, back up for a second... John Locke...

TOM   ...established the concept of the social contract, by theorizing that in a state of nature, some of man's natural rights must be sacrificed so that most other natural rights can be upheld through the consent to be governed.

WHITCOMB	Excuse me?
TOM	John Locke established the concept of the social contract by theorizing that in a state of nature
WHITCOMB	How do you know?
TOM	Ron told me.
WHITCOMB	Ron?
TOM	Yeah.
WHITCOMB	Um... look, Tom, I don't want to trouble you any longer than necessary, and we've got a lot to do, so could we just get started? Please?
TOM	Oh, sure... What do we have to do?

Whitcomb takes a seat at the table, opens his briefcase, and spreads out his work: piles and piles of official documents.

WHITCOMB	Well, Tom, I'm just going to ask you to answer a few simple questions, alright?
TOM	Alright.
WHITCOMB	Name?
TOM	Hm?
WHITCOMB	Your full name? What is it?
TOM	Tom. You knew that.
WHITCOMB	[*groaning and writing*] 'Mr... Thomas... Doe...' Okay, now what is your yearly income?
TOM	My yearly income?
WHITCOMB	That's right. [*Tom doesn't understand.*] How much money did you make this year?
TOM	Oh... um... none.

Five Visits from Mr Whitcomb

WHITCOMB None?

TOM Nope.

WHITCOMB [*a brief pause*] None?

TOM Nope.

WHITCOMB Oh... Okay... None?

TOM Nope.

WHITCOMB Well, I guess that's a relief, then, because if you don't make any money, you don't have to pay any taxes.

TOM So that means...

WHITCOMB Well, if you don't have to pay taxes, then I won't be bothering you any more.

TOM You're leaving?

Whitcomb starts packing up his papers.

WHITCOMB I'm leaving.

TOM Okay. Bye. [*Whitcomb opens the door and starts to leave.*] Oh, wait, there was one thing. [*Whitcomb stops.*] Last spring I swept Mr. Harley's porch for a quarter. You know Mr. Harley? 'Harley's General Store' in Beanville? Well, I needed a goldfish bowl, because I had just met Ron and the only place he had to stay was in a hollow tree stump filled with rainwater and

WHITCOMB Wait a second... This man paid you? Real money?

TOM A quarter. I don't know, I never even saw the quarter, because this bowl cost a quarter, so it was an even swap, because, like I said, Ron needed a place to stay, and

WHITCOMB Tom, if Mr. Harley paid you for your services, then that counts as income.

TOM Oh, okay, so should I

WHITCOMB Furthermore, I think it my duty to remind you that I am a duly appointed official of the United States Government, and withholding such vital information from me can be considered a federal offense. However, considering your relative ignorance of the matter, I'll let it slide this time.

TOM I'm sorry... I just forgot, that's all...

WHITCOMB That's quite alright, Tom...[*he whips out a pocket calculator*] Now, for a yearly income of point-2-5 dollars, with one animal dependant, no mortgage, no social security... [*he starts mumbling to himself, before reaching the final calculation.*] Okay, according to my calculator, you owe the Government... 5.2 cents. Treasury guidelines allow us to round that off to five cents. [*grinning*] What do you say, Tom? One nickel?

TOM I -- I don't have it.

WHITCOMB You don't have it... Oh, come on! Just one nickel! You don't have five cents laying around somewhere?

TOM No.

WHITCOMB [*groaning*] I see. Well, will Mr. Harley let you sweep the porch again?

TOM He has an assistant who does that now. I'd love to help you, Mr. Whitcomb. I'd love to help the government. I just don't have the money.

WHITCOMB Tom, taxes aren't charitable donations. You have to pay them. It's the law.

TOM So - so what do I do?

WHITCOMB Well, there's really only one plausible solution. We'll have to repossess the fishbowl. Now in most cases like this...

TOM [*to Ron*] What? No, Ron... No, they won't... Ron, don't worry, they...

WHITCOMB ...the Treasury Department will offer a low-interest loan in order to help you to regain financial stability. However...

TOM Ron, please don't scream... It's alright...

WHITCOMB ...in order to regain ownership of repossessed property, you'll have to file a writ of--

TOM Ron says you can't have his bowl.

WHITCOMB	Well, I'm afraid there's no other way... Wait - Ron says I can't have it?
TOM	Uh huh.
WHITCOMB	[*thinking*] Tom, what if I were to come back tomorrow, and bring along a friend of mine, a doctor? Would you be willing to talk to her for a few minutes?
TOM	Okay.
WHITCOMB	Good. Why don't I go call her right now?
TOM	That's a good idea, because I've actually got some work to do. I have to [*referring to his list*] weed the garden, eat, feed the fish...
WHITCOMB	Right. Well... I'll see you tomorrow, Tom.
TOM	Bye, Mr. Whitcomb. [*Whitcomb exits. Tom watches him out the window, then turns to Ron*] What? No, I think he's a nice guy.

Blackout. A harsh spot up on Whitcomb. He is talking on a cellular phone.

WHITCOMB	[*very serious*] Hello, Dr. Benton? I think we've got an extremely aberrant tax evader on our hands here...

Visit No. 2

Lights come up. It is morning again in the cabin. Tom is standing at the window.

TOM	What?... [*He turns to Ron*] Yeah. [*He continues to look out the window. He then turns back again.*] What? Yeah, I suppose you're right. [*He leaves his post at the window, and goes over to the table, sits down and starts writing.*] Okay... 'Things to do today: Number one, weed the garden. Number two, eat. Number three, feed the fish -' [*A knock is heard at the door.*] Hey... there's that knocking sound again. [*Three more knocks.*] I forget, did we ever figure out where that was coming from? [*Three more exasperated knocks.*] What?... Oh, yeah! Mr. Whitcomb! I forgot!

Opens the door, and Whitcomb enters, along with Dr. Benton, a psychologist.

WHITCOMB	Hi, Tom. Remember me?

TOM   Mr. Whitcomb. It's nice to see you again.

WHITCOMB   Tom, this is my friend, Dr. Benton.

BENTON   How do you do, Tom?

TOM   I'm fine... Oh, this is Ron. My fish.

WHITCOMB   [*whispering to Benton*] This is what I was talking about. Watch, he'll start talking to it.

TOM   So you're a doctor?

BENTON   That's right.

TOM   What field?

BENTON   [*with a slight uneasiness*] Criminal Psychology.

TOM   [*unfazed*] Behavioural or analytical?

BENTON   Excuse me?

TOM   Do you practice psychology with a behavioural or an analytical approach?

BENTON   Both.

TOM   Oh.

BENTON   [*whispering to Whitcomb*] I don't see anything wrong with him.

WHITCOMB   [*whispering*] Ask him more!

BENTON   Tom, do you know the difference between behavioral and analytical psychology?

TOM   What, you don't know? I thought you're a doctor?

BENTON   Of course I know...

TOM   Then what are you asking me for?

BENTON   I'm... I'm interested in knowing... whether or not you know.

Five Visits from Mr Whitcomb

TOM   Why are you so interested?

BENTON   Because it's my job.

TOM   I thought your job was Criminal Psychologist

BENTON   LOOK, DO YOU TALK TO YOUR FISH OR DON'T YOU???

A moment of abrupt silence.

TOM   Yes.

WHITCOMB   Ah-ha!

TOM   Why, what does that have to do with - ?

BENTON   Tom, if you don't mind, I'd like to ask you a few questions.

TOM   Oh yeah, questions. Mr. Whitcomb was asking me questions yesterday.

BENTON   Yes, well these questions might be a little bit different. You might wish to make yourself more comfortable. Perhaps you'd like to lie down on the bed?

TOM   If you say so...

He lies down on the bed. Benton pulls a chair up next to him.

BENTON   Now, Tom... Could you please tell me about your relationship with Ron?

TOM   We're friends.

BENTON   How long have you known him?

TOM   Um... We met last spring. You see, I live by this big river, and sometimes, the rapids splash water way up onto the shore, making all these little pools wedged in between the rocks. Anyway, I was walking along the bank, and I looked down, and there he was, swimming in this little pool. So I said, 'Hello.' and he said 'Hello.' and I said 'What are you doing in there?' and he said 'I was thrown from the rapids.' and I said 'Do you want me to put you back in the river?' and he said 'No, I like it here' and I said 'Why?' and he said 'Because there's no rapids and no sharp rocks in here.' and I said 'Why don't you come live with me?' and he said 'Are there any rapids or sharp rocks where you live?' and I said 'No.' and he said 'Okay' and so now he lives with me.

BENTON I see. And where did you get the name 'Ron'?

TOM He told it to me.

BENTON I see. And where did he get the name 'Ron'?

TOM [*gives her a look like she's an idiot, but in a nice way*] I assume his parents gave it to him.

BENTON I see. And where did his parents get the name 'Ron'?

TOM I don't know. You'd have to ask them. His real name's Ronald though.

BENTON Ronald?

TOM Yeah, but you can call him Ron for short.

WHITCOMB Kind of like Tom is short for Thomas.

TOM Uh... No, my name is Tom. Just Tom.

BENTON Tom, could you excuse me for a moment? I need to see Mr. Whitcomb privately.

TOM Okay... Did I- Did I do alright?

BENTON Oh, you did fine, Tom. Don't worry. I wasn't testing you or anything like that. There were no right or wrong answers to any of those questions.

TOM [*relieved*] Oh.

Benton takes Whitcomb over into a corner.

WHITCOMB Well?

BENTON This is far more serious than I expected.

WHITCOMB Oh boy...

BENTON Tom is a classic case of aberrant sociopathic dysfunction, severely inclined to schizophrenia and kleptomania.

Five Visits from Mr Whitcomb

WHITCOMB So you're saying...

BENTON He's nuts.

WHITCOMB I knew it...

BENTON Yes, I'm afraid Tom is a walking time bomb, really, a master criminal under the guise of 'the introverted simpleton'. His relationship with this fish reveals something... diabolical about his subconscious mind, a sort of paranoid psychopathia, making his condition extremely dangerous.

WHITCOMB Dangerous? You mean ...

BENTON I mean that what begins with tax evasion today could lead to worse crimes tomorrow, crimes like rape, incest, and even murder.

WHITCOMB Oh my God... I mean, not that any of those are any worse than tax evasion, but... What do you recommend we do?

BENTON I'm afraid Tom will have to be installed in a mental facility where proper tests can be conducted, proper incarceration can be arranged, and if nessecary, proper... surgical correction can be applied.

WHITCOMB Whoa, wait a second... I can't let you do that, Doctor.

BENTON Mr. Whitcomb, Tom's condition can't be remedied with simple psychotropic drugs. Only through intensive neurological surgery can we --

WHITCOMB No, no, no, I don't care about that... I'm talking about this 'incarceration' thing. In case you didn't realise, this is a federal matter, and since Tom has a debt to pay to the United States Government, if anyone's going to lock him up, it'll be in a federal penitentiary.

BENTON This is not some common criminal we're dealing with here!

WHITCOMB I'm sorry, Doctor, but I will not compromise my duty to the United States of America.

BENTON Let me have him on weekends.

WHITCOMB Once a month.

BENTON Plus holidays.

WHITCOMB	Sold.
BENTON	[*turning back to Tom, who's been oblivious to the entire conversation*] Tom?
TOM	Yes?
WHITCOMB	Listen, Tom... Dr. Benton and I were wondering if you'd like to take a little trip with us.
TOM	A trip?
BENTON	Tom, since you haven't paid your taxes, we need you to come with us to a place called 'Washington', where we'll go to this building, called a 'Federal Courthouse', where you'll meet a friend of ours, called 'the judge'. And if 'the judge' says you can come back here, then you can come back here and never be bothered by us again.
WHITCOMB	...until next year's income tax.
BENTON	What do you say, Tom.
TOM	[*a long, pensive pause*] Would I be able to bring Ron?
WHITCOMB	Absolutely.
TOM	Would there be food for us?
BENTON	We'd cover all the expenses.
TOM	[*listening to Ron for a moment*] Would I be able to reserve the right to council?
WHITCOMB	Sure.
TOM	Um... I'm sorry, I don't think I can.
BENTON	You don't think you can?
TOM	Ron would get homesick, and besides, I have to weed my garden every morning. Sorry.
WHITCOMB	Tom, I don't think you quite understand.
BENTON	[*interrupting him*] Alright, Tom. That's fine. If you don't want to leave, then we won't make you. Whatever you want is just fine with us. We're your friends,

		Tom. We care about you.
	TOM	Oh... really? You, you mean that?
	BENTON	Of course we do, Tom.
	TOM	Um... thanks.
	BENTON	We'll be going now, Tom... Goodbye, Tom.
	TOM	Goodbye, Dr. Benton.
	WHITCOMB	Bye, Tom.
	TOM	Goodbye, Mr. Whitcomb.

They both leave. Lights down. Spotlight on Whitcomb and Benton outside the house.

WHITCOMB		What was that all about? We can't just leave him here!
BENTON		Don't worry, Mr. Whitcomb. We'll come back later... with the Law...

Visit No. 3

It is the afternoon. The cabin is empty. A knock is heard. A pause and then another. Another pause, and then another knock.

WHITCOMB	Tom, are you in there? Tom! [*He barges in.*] Tom, from now on, whenever you hear that knocking sound, would you please - [*He sees that the room is empty.*] Where is he?

Dr. Benton follows him in, followed by the Sheriff, a large, burly man in a classic Northwest Sheriff's uniform.

BENTON	He must have known we would come back for him. It all makes perfect sense.
SHERIFF	I still can't believe this is Tom we're talking about.
WHITCOMB	His fishbowl's gone! Does that mean anything, Doctor?
BENTON	Let's hope not.

SHERIFF I mean, Tom was always the most pleasant boy. I can't imagine him being some common criminal.

BENTON Tom is far from a mere common criminal, Sheriff. He's a deviant.

SHERIFF Maybe he is a... a deviant, but that doesn't change the fact that he's such a nice guy. I mean, I've only met him a few times, but from those few times, I can honestly tell you I have never met a kinder, gentler ...

WHITCOMB [*scanning the Sheriff's belt*] Sheriff, where's your gun?

SHERIFF My gun?

WHITCOMB For God's sake, man, do you think this is some game? This is a potentially dangerous criminal we're dealing with! What kind of a law enforcement officer doesn't bring a sidearm when apprehending a suspect?

SHERIFF I- I didn't think Tom was a ...

WHITCOMB I knew I should have brought Federal troops. I just knew it.

BENTON Where could he be? Do you have any idea, Sheriff?

SHERIFF I really couldn't tell you. Like I said, the only times I ever see him are when he comes into Beanville now and again. Like last Spring when he needed that fishbowl.

WHITCOMB Has he had a previous criminal record that you know of?

SHERIFF Haven't you been listening to me? I'm telling you, Tom would never hurt a fly. Whenever he comes into town, he talks to the old ladies, he throws a baseball around with the kids. He even helps people carry groceries, and picks up litter off the street. For no reason other than basic human goodness. I'm sorry, Mr. Whitcomb... I think you have the wrong man.

WHITCOMB The wrong man.

SHERIFF That's right.

WHITCOMB Just what are you trying to imply, Sheriff? Are you questioning my competence as an auditor? Are you saying we should let him off the hook because he's a nice guy?

Five Visits from Mr Whitcomb

SHERIFF   No, all I'm saying ...

WHITCOMB   Sheriff, in my twenty-one years as an agent of the IRS, I have brought no less than 134 suspects of tax evasion to justice. 134! And if I gave a tax break to every nice guy that came along with a good sob story or a sincere looking grin, then that would be 134 criminals walking the street today thanks to my negligence.

SHERIFF   I didn't mean to--

WHITCOMB   Twenty-one years ago I took an oath, Sheriff, an oath by which I swore to uphold the contitutional government of the United States of America through the execution of the duties of my appointed post at all costs! I am a servant of the people, Sheriff! I am a soldier, a knight, marching for the cause of freedom and democracy through economic providence! I will not forgo the responsibilities of my office, even if it means nice guys have to suffer! I will not compromise the United States of America, whether it's for a nickel or for two hundred million dollars! As John Adams, one of our great founding forefathers, once declared, 'I have sworn upon the altar of God eternal hostility against every form of tyranny over the mind of man!!!'

He stops, panting and gasping for air. Nobody notices Tom, standing in the doorway, holding Ron's fishbowl in one hand, and a rifle in the other.

TOM   That was Jefferson who said that.

Everyone turns and gasps.

BENTON   Oh my God, he's got a gun.

TOM   Oh, yeah, we were just doing some hunting.

WHITCOMB   We don't want any trouble, Tom.

TOM   [*going over to the table and sitting down*] Oh, don't mind me. I was just about to [*recalling his list*] eat.

Whitcomb draws Benton and the Sheriff into a huddle.

WHITCOMB   Okay, we've got to think fast.

BENTON   We could try to overpower him, get the gun away from him.

WHITCOMB: Too risky. Of course we wouldn't be in this crisis if this dimwit had brought his gun!

SHERIFF: Dimwit? Who's the dimwit here? He hasn't even threatened us yet! I can't believe you two are so worried. I say we just walk on out.

BENTON: Jesus, Sheriff, what kind of a cop are you? How can you not see the grave danger of this situation! We are in a room with a psychologically deranged man with a shotgun!

WHITCOMB: Maybe... maybe we could reason with him, convince him to let us live.

BENTON: That's risky. But I guess we don't have many options left.

SHERIFF: Now, just wait a second...

WHITCOMB: You'd better do the talking, Doctor.

BENTON: You're right. Okay, now let's all just stay calm. We don't want to upset him in any way. Ready? Here we go. [*They all turn around to Tom*] Tom? [*She approaches him slowly, carefully.*] Can you hear me, Tom?

TOM: Sure I can hear you.

BENTON: Please... Is Tom in there? I want to speak... to Tom...

TOM: [*confused, almost suspicious*] This is Tom speaking.

BENTON: Tom... Listen to me Tom... You don't want to do anything you may regret later...

TOM: Okay...

BENTON: We're your friends, Tom. We don't want to hurt you. We care about you, Tom.

TOM: Really? Do, do you mean that?

BENTON: Of course I do, Tom. Of course I do. And right now, we're going to walk out that door, and we won't bother you any more. How does that sound? Is that alright with you Tom?

TOM: Actually, yeah, that's a good idea, because I still have to [*referring to his list*] eat, then feed the fish, then--

Five Visits from Mr Whitcomb 43

He puts the rifle down on the table.

WHITCOMB [*in a sudden outburst*] Let's go! Now!!!

The three of them run for their lives, stumbling over each other to get out the door. In a flash, they are gone, and Tom and Ron are alone.

TOM -- weed the garden, then eat, then ...

He looks around, shrugs. Blackout.

Visit No. 4.

It is now night. Tom lies asleep on the bed. Suddenly, he lunges upward, waking with a start.

TOM What was that?... [*He lights a candle.*] Ron, did you hear that?... I don't know... It sounded like... voices... and footsteps... in the woods...

He very slowly gets out of bed, and calmly walks over to the window to look outside. He looks out for a moment, yawns, stretches, scratches, when suddenly... GUNSHOTS! The rattle of semi-automatic booms from outside the cabin, as the interior is sprayed with bullets. Miraculously, Tom manages to run to the table, grab Ron, and hide under the bed, all the while narrowly escaping death. The gunshots end quickly. The voice of a Federal Agent booms over a megaphone.

FED. [*off*] Mr. Thomas Doe! Mr. Thomas Doe! We know you're in there, Mr. Doe! Your cabin is surrounded! Come out now, and nobody gets hurt!

TOM [*scared out of his wits*] GO AWAY!

FED. [*off*] We're not going to play games, Mr. Doe!

TOM LEAVE ME ALONE!

FED. [*off*] We'll leave you alone when you let those innocent people leave safely!

TOM WHAT INNOCENT PEOPLE???

FED. [*after a short pause*] Okay, we're willing to listen to your demands.

TOM   I DEMAND THAT YOU LEAVE ME ALONE!

FED.   [*off*] No can do, I'm afraid. Not until you let those people go.

TOM   WHAT PEOPLE ???

FED.   [*another short pause. We hear the Federal Agent yelling to the troops, without the megaphone*] Wait, he does have hostages, doesn't he? [*Over the megaphone*] You do have hostages, don't you?

TOM   NO!!!

FED.   [*off the megaphone*] Well, for crying out loud - who told me he had hostages? Somebody said something... [*On the megaphone*] Are you sure there's nobody else in there?

TOM   WELL, I'VE GOT A FISH...

FED.   [*on the megaphone*] Well, you let that fish go right now, Mister, or there'll be hell to pay!

TOM   NO, YOU DON'T UNDERSTAND

FED.   [*on the megaphone*] Don't make us come in there! We'll give you the count of three... One...

TOM   OH GOD!

FED.   [*on the megaphone*] Two... [*off the megaphone*] Wait a second... Did he just say 'Oh God'? Tell me he didn't just say 'Oh God'... [*on the megaphone*] Did you just say 'Oh God'?

TOM   YEAH...

FED.   [*off the megaphone*] Great... [*on the megaphone*] Okay, look, if you have any prophecies you want to read over the radio, or something like that, I have no problem with it. But frankly, if you think you can - Wait, hold on a second... [*Off the megaphone*] Who are you?

WHITCOMB   [*off*]Whitcomb. Treasury Department.

TOM   MR. WHITCOMB???

Five Visits from Mr Whitcomb

WHITCOMB   TOM, IS THAT YOU???

FED.   [*off the megaphone*] Wait, use this.

WHITCOMB   [*on the megaphone*] Hello, Tom.

TOM   WHAT IS GOING ON???

WHITCOMB   You have to pay your taxes!

TOM   I DON'T UNDERSTAND!!!

WHITCOMB   You see, Tom, the government is like a business...

TOM   I KNOW! I KNOW!

WHITCOMB   We don't want to hurt you, Tom!

TOM   DON'T WANT TO HURT ME??? [*He stands up and looks out the window*] DON'T WANT TO - [*Gunshots ring out again, spraying the cabin once more. Tom dives back under the bed*] I CAN'T TALK TO YOU THIS WAY! COME IN HERE!

WHITCOMB   In... In the cabin?... Now?

TOM   YES, NOW!!!

WHITCOMB   Um... Well... Okay... Everybody hold your fire! I'm -- I'm going in!

There is a silence. Tom realises he's got a safe moment, so he acts fast: grabbing his gun off the table, and loading it just as Whitcomb walks in the door.

TOM   [*fuming, holding him at gunpoint*] Ron says you lied to me.

WHITCOMB   I told you, you had to pay your taxes. And you refused.

TOM   Ron says I haven't done anything wrong. He says so. He says the only reason this is happening is because you're an evil man.

WHITCOMB   Tom, don't get the wrong impression.

TOM   He says your whole life is one big power trip. He says you go around, taking people's money, and using the United States of America to feel powerful, to feel omnipotent. He says you can't stand to see someone living out in the woods, never bothering anyone and never having reason to complain, so you had to just come and wreck all of it...

WHITCOMB Tom, I am a servant of the people! I am committed to a cause, and if you think my reasons for doing what I do are in the slightest bit selfish, then I'm afraid you're sorely mistaken.

TOM Ron says--

WHITCOMB Ron is no concern of mine, Tom. You are. Now pay your taxes.

TOM I can't.

WHITCOMB Then you're going to jail.

TOM I'm not going anywhere.

WHITCOMB Then you'll die.

TOM [*he cocks the gun*] Then we'll die.

Whitcomb is spooked. Tom is icy.

WHITCOMB Tom... Please understand... this is my life, Tom... This is everything I believe in...

TOM 'All great changes are irksome to the human mind, especially those which are attended with great dangers and uncertain effects.'

WHITCOMB Locke?

TOM John Adams.

WHITCOMB When did you get so smart?

TOM You don't know me, Mr. Whitcomb.

They stare at each other for a moment. Then, without a word, Tom picks up the fishbowl and hands it to Whitcomb. Whitcomb accepts it, though slightly shocked. Tom turns and looks away.
Whitcomb is frozen. Finally, he starts to move towards the door, but then stops again. Looking back at Tom for a moment, he walks over to the table, and sets the bowl back down. Then, silently, he leaves the cabin. The lights fade to black.

Visit No. 5

The lights rise again slowly. It is morning. Tom is standing at the window, looking out. Ron says nothing to him. Finally, he goes to sit down at the table.

TOM   Okay... [*writing*] 'Things to do today: Number one, weed the garden. Number two, eat. Number three, [*he gazes longingly at Ron for a moment*] feed the fish.' [*A knock is heard at the door, three raps in perfect succession. Tom looks up. He is scared. Three more raps are heard. He rises, grabs his gun, and opens the door. It is Whitcomb.*]

WHITCOMB   Hi, Tom.

TOM   Hi.

Tom walks back to the table, but does not sit down. Whitcomb lets himself in, visibly uncomfortable.

WHITCOMB   How are you?

TOM   Fine.

WHITCOMB   And how's Ron?

TOM   Why don't you ask him?

WHITCOMB   Um... okay... How are you, Ron? [*He is puzzled, expecting an answer from Tom. Finally, he fills it in for himself.*] Oh. That's good to hear.

TOM   He didn't say anything.

WHITCOMB   Oh... Of course.

TOM   He hasn't spoken in a week.

WHITCOMB   Really? How come?

TOM   [*with melancholic sarcasm*] Fish can't talk. [*Pause*] Why are you here?

WHITCOMB   I just wanted to let you know that your taxes are all taken care of. You don't owe anything more.

TOM   Who paid?

WHITCOMB	I did.
TOM	Well, thank you very much. Now if you don't mind, I've got to weed the garden.
WHITCOMB	That's not all, Tom. I also wanted to say that... I'm really sorry about this. If there's anything I can do, anything at all...
TOM	You could leave.
WHITCOMB	Yeah... [*He starts to leave, stops.*] I didn't mean to change you, Tom.
TOM	Change me?
WHITCOMB	I didn't mean for it to turn out this way. I didn't mean for Ron to stop talking to you. I was... just doing my job.
TOM	That's an excuse for war criminals.
WHITCOMB	See, that was sarcastic. You're not a sarcastic person, Tom.
TOM	[*sarcastically*] Oh, I'm not, am I?
WHITCOMB	Tom, can't you just forget? Can't you just forget any of this ever happened, and get on with life? I can't live with myself knowing what I've done. Just... please, try to forget, Tom.
TOM	That's Mr. Doe to you.

Whitcomb turns to the fishbowl.

WHITCOMB	Ron... Ron, say something! Please, talk some sense into him! He- he doesn't belong in the rapids, Ron... There's too many sharp rocks! It's dangerous! Please, talk to him! Say something! [*Ron speaks.*] Fine, tell him that!... Whatever... Well don't talk to me about it - tell him!... Of course I am!
TOM	That's really funny, Mr. Whitcomb, but it won't work. I told you -- [*Ron cuts him off.*] Ron!... Yes... No... Of course not... I'm sorry...
WHITCOMB	That's it, Ron... You tell him...
TOM	You're right... [*looking up at Whitcomb*] I accept your apology, Mr. Whitcomb... And so does Ron.

WHITCOMB [*collecting himself*] Oh. Okay...

TOM Now, um, if you don't mind, I have to weed the garden, then eat, then feed the fish...

WHITCOMB So that's it?

TOM What's it?

WHITCOMB You forgive me? You've forgotten? It's all over?

TOM Sure.

WHITCOMB Well then... [*becoming official once more*] Tom, the Internal Revenue Service thanks you for your cooperation.

TOM No problem.

Pause. Whitcomb begins to leave, then stops.

WHITCOMB You will forget this, won't you, Tom?

TOM Forget what?

WHITCOMB [*smiling, turning out the door*] Nothing. Never mind.

TOM Mr. Whitcomb?

WHITCOMB Yes?

TOM You won't forget this, will you?

WHITCOMB Not a chance.

The lights go dark, but a spot remains on Whitcomb, on the other side of the cabin door. He starts to leave, but stops. He has to make sure it's all erased. He turns back to the door, and knocks on it, three raps in perfect succession. As he does this, another spot comes up on Tom, sitting at the table in rapt communion with Ron. He pays no attention to the knocking. Whitcomb knocks again, and again, there is no response. He knocks once more, and then turns, smiles, and drifts off into the darkness. Tom looks up suddenly.

TOM Did you hear something?

Blackout.

THE END

Skin

NEIL BISWAS

Neil Biswas was born in London in 1971. He is a graduate in English Literature from Oxford University and has had several plays produced in Britain, including *Skin* which was performed by the Soho Theatre Company in London in January 1994. He has written a libretto for the English National Opera's Baylis Programme and is currently writing a play for BBC Radio 3.

Skin

CHARACTERS

    MRS AURAUTI SEN, *Bengali. Forty-five years old.*
    SUMITA SEN, *Bengali. Twenty-one years old.*
    MR BHOSE, *Bengali. Fifty years old.*
    MRS MINAKI BHOSE, *Bengali. Forty-five years old.*

SETTING

The stage is split into two sections: the living room and the kitchen. When the characters are speaking in the living room, the kitchen is unlit, and vice versa, Except for the light the projector sheds on the screen in the living room, which is always on.

Scene One

The kitchen. Table with food. Sumita and Mrs Sen prepare food.

SUMITA	Where's the daal?
Mrs SEN	Behind you.
SUMITA	Do you want to use these bowls?
Mrs SEN	No use the new ones in the right cupboard.
SUMITA	When did you get these?
Mrs SEN	I bought them last week.
SUMITA	Oh yeah?
Mrs SEN	The old ones are so faded.

Sumita picks up an old bowl and examines it. Mrs Sen turns around to look at her.

Mrs SEN	Will you pour the tea, dear.
SUMITA	OK.
Mrs SEN	How many lucchis do you want?

SUMITA	I don't know-not many. One or two.	
Mrs SEN	Have some more.	
SUMITA	Two will be fine.	
Mrs SEN	You're not dieting are you...you're already so thin.	
SUMITA	[*loudly*] Two will be fine. [*Pause.*] Besides, Bhose cacoo will eat his usual fifteen.	
MRS SEN	[*to herself*] Not any more.	
SUMITA	You should have bought a new teapot too.	
Mrs SEN	Why?	
SUMITA	Because this one's crap.	
Mrs SEN	Sumita!	
SUMITA	Where's the sugar?	
Mrs SEN	Darling, you know where the sugar is--you've only been away three months..	

Mrs Sen turns to face Sumita's back. Sumita stands still.

Left cupboard, next to the coffee.

Sumita finds the sugar. Slams it on the tray.

What's the matter, dear?

SUMITA	Why, mum?	
Mrs SEN	What, dear?	
SUMITA	Why have you invited them?	
Mrs SEN	Come on, Sumita.	
SUMITA	Tell me..	

Skin 53

    Mrs SEN   You know why, dear.

Scene Two

In the sitting room, Mr Bhose gets up and examines the projector.

    Mrs BHOSE   Don't touch it. You'll break it.

    Mr BHOSE   Don't be stupid. Mohanda and I spent a long time playing with this. Splicing..Cutting..Editing.

    Mrs BHOSE   Editing-Smediting. Sit down.

    Mr BHOSE   We were proper film makers--like Truffaut, Fellini, Satyajit Ray...'Documentors of Life'.

    Mrs BHOSE   You talk such rubbish. Neither of you could hold the camera still.

    Mr BHOSE   That's not true. We were perfecting our own style of images.

    Mrs BHOSE   Most of the time you took pictures of our feet.

Slight pause.

    Mr BHOSE   [*with a big smile*] Ah..but you have such lovely feet.

    Mrs BHOSE   What? [*She looks down.*] Be quiet you big fool.

Sumita comes in with a tea tray, and Indian sweets.

    Mr BHOSE   Fine.

    SUMITA   Mummy bought some Jelabees specially for you Bhose cacoo.

    Mr BHOSE   Ah...Jelabees--the mere sound of--

    Mrs BHOSE   She shouldn't have. His doctor forbids rich things.

    SUMITA   Surely not all the time.

    SUMITA   We could have done this on our own. Just the two of us.

    Mrs SEN   So why haven't we?

Lights down on the kitchen and up in the sitting room. Four chairs, coffee table, a projector in the middle of the room, facing a screen. Mr and Mrs Bhose are sitting.

Mrs BHOSE   Your shirt's hanging out.

Mr BHOSE   It's loose. Freestyle.

Mrs BHOSE   Tuck it in.

Mr BHOSE   The Sen's have seen my belly before.

He looks at her.

Mr BHOSE   OK. OK. There. Neat and tidy.

Mrs BHOSE   It's a new carpet?

Mr BHOSE   I can't remember. When did we last come...puja two years ago?

Mrs BHOSE   No we came for Sumita's twenty-first birthday last year.

Mrs BHOSE   It's good that she's bought something new.

Mr BHOSE   [*looking around*] It's a nice house. Small, but nice.

-Mrs BHOSE   What would she do with a big house?

Mr BHOSE   Exactly. Listen to our Sumita. She's a well-educated student of... of...

SUMITA   Sociology.

Mr BHOSE   Sociology. She knows much better than these tin-pot doctors. Sit down next to me Sumita, so you've started a job.

SUMITA   In Manchester.

Mrs BHOSE   Are you alright so far away from home?

SUMITA   It's an exciting city.

Mr BHOSE   We're very proud of you. Researching--yes?

SUMITA   Uh-huh.

Mr BHOSE You'll soon be telling us how to improve our lives.

Mrs BHOSE What point would there be in telling you. You would still sit there.

Mr BHOSE Oh shut up, woman. I tell you Sumita, English husbands talk about being henpecked--they know nothing of the pneumatic drill every Bengali wife carries with her.

SUMITA [*laughs*] How's Bobby?

Mrs BHOSE He's decided to do an M.A.

SUMITA Really? Oh, where's he doing it?

Mrs BHOSE He's staying in London.

SUMITA He told me he wanted to go to Liverpool.

Mrs BHOSE No, the department's much better here.

Mr BHOSE You look very thin, Sumita. Are you sure you are doing enough cooking?

SUMITA I cook all the time, cacoo.

Mrs BHOSE Your mother says you're living in a very rough area.

SUMITA Hulme? No, it's alright. You just have to know where not to go.

Mr BHOSE Our Sumita's as tough as anyone, aren't you dear?

SUMITA I suppose.

Mrs BHOSE Is Ma coping on her own?

SUMITA I think so.

Mrs BHOSE It must be hard to do everything only for yourself.

SUMITA [*loudly*] She's alright.

Mr BHOSE Of course she is, Sumita, and proud that her daughter is doing so well.

SUMITA   Thank you, cacoo.

Mrs Sen comes in with the food. Mrs Bhose gets up to help her.

Mr BHOSE   Lucchi-Kebabs. Fan-tastic. Grand. Take note dear how I'm treated in other people's houses.

Mrs Sen looks at Mr Bhose.

Mrs SEN   I've forgotten the chutney.

She rushes back to the kitchen.

Mrs BHOSE   Hold on, Aurauti...

Mrs Bhose follows her. Lights down on sitting room, up on kitchen.

Aurauti dear, are you alright?

Mrs SEN   It's here somewhere. I put it down just a minute ago.

Mrs BHOSE   Look at me, Aurauti.

Mrs SEN   Well...

Mrs BHOSE   We don't have to watch them, you know.

Mrs SEN   It's just Bhoseda's face...I'm being silly.

Mrs BHOSE   Aurauti...

Mrs SEN   Do you think I've made enough lucchis?

Mrs BHOSE   Yes.

Mrs Sen picks up the chutney. It's right in front of her.

Mrs SEN   Oh, it was here all the time.

Mrs BHOSE   Of course.

Mrs SEN   You know me too well.

Skin

Mrs BHOSE Did you hear what I said, Aurauti, we don't have to...

Mrs SEN I heard...Suleka, we do have to do it. I have to do it.

Mrs BHOSE Are you ready for this?

Mrs SEN For five years I've been hiding...

Mrs BHOSE From the past?

Mrs SEN No. The future. I think it's time for me to open my eyes.

Mrs BHOSE What about Sumita?

Mrs SEN She'll be alright.

Mrs BHOSE She seems very edgy.

Mrs SEN They're just films. Moving photos...I know that.

Mrs BHOSE Bhose is under the impression that they're masterpieces.

They both laugh.

Mrs SEN How is he?

Mrs BHOSE You know him, he thinks he's Superman. But the doctor thinks otherwise.

Mrs SEN Oh.

Mrs BHOSE He gives Bhose a solid telling off every time he goes.

Mrs SEN It's what he needs.

Mrs BHOSE [*laughing*] I know. He's such a little boy at heart.

Mrs SEN They all are.

Mrs BHOSE Too much James Bond, no?

They laugh. Lights down on kitchen. Lights up on sitting room.

Mr BHOSE   Our brides were still in Calcutta. We were living in this pokey little room-Mohanda would always keep his clothes in the suitcase.

SUMITA   Why?

Mr BHOSE   Heaven knows. He flatly refused to unpack.

SUMITA   How strange.

Mr BHOSE   Exactly. I think he felt that if something went wrong, or he missed his mother's cooking too much...Straight back to Calcutta -- 'jawa' -- no fuss. No wait.

Sumita laughs.

Mr BHOSE   He would always say 'Bai, make sure you look at me every evening--take a good look -- tell me if this cold weather is making me go pale -- 'forshah' -- if it is we must go quickstep back for a 'top up'.

Bhose laughs. He notices that Sumita is not laughing.

Sumita?

SUMITA   He went back for his 'top up' didn't he?

Mr BHOSE   What?

SUMITA   But not to Calcutta.

Pause. Sumita turns to Bhose.

Without a thought, he left us.

Mr BHOSE   No, Sumita.

SUMITA   Without thinking about anyone. Just himself.

Mr BHOSE   Don't talk like this, Sumita.

SUMITA   Why not! It's true. We were supposed to carry on without asking...just look how Ma became.

Mr BHOSE   You mustn't blame ...

SUMITA	Is this what he wanted for her? To stay in the house for three years, not speaking to anyone. Doing puja to him three times a day--refusing to eat at certain times, unless I made her.
Mr BHOSE	Your mother ...
SUMITA	Tell me Bhose cacoo, did he know he was doing this?
Mr BHOSE	Please don't hurt yourself, little one.
SUMITA	I'm not little, anymore....all that talk of what we were going to do. His plans..so much nonsense. Why did he say those things if...
Mr BHOSE	Sumita.
SUMITA	[*slowly*] He didn't care.
Mr BHOSE	Of course he did.
SUMITA	He didn't even wait...wait for me to...

Mrs Sen and Mrs Bhose return.

MRS SEN	What's the matter?
SUMITA	Nothing. Nothing at all.

Pause. Sumita turns to face the wall. Mrs Sen sits down.

Mrs BHOSE	Aurauti, do you want some water?
Mrs SEN	Thank you.
Mrs BHOSE	This chutney is very nice
Mr BHOSE	Home made bliss.
Mrs SEN	Thank you.
Mrs SEN	Bhoseda, I hear you have bought a 'jommie' in Calcutta.
Mr BHOSE	Oh yes, it's in Laketown. We're hoping to build a two-storey flat on it.

Mrs BHOSE	It's always hoping. It's taken him twenty-five years to buy this bit of wasteland.
Mr BHOSE	It's a top class jommie.
Mrs SEN	You retire next year, don't you?
Mr BHOSE	Who knows, the way they are talking to me I think they've made my goldwatch early..the English are at their most charming when they say 'goodbye' -- 'bari jow' my good friend. Go home now.
Mrs SEN	And Bobby?
Mrs BHOSE	Bobby's going to complete his studies here and then who knows, he'll probably marry some hippy girl who likes dark men.
Mr BHOSE	As long as she can cook, I don't care if she smokes gaja all day...so what films are we going to watch?

Mrs Sen looks at Sumita, who is still facing away.

Mrs SEN	Sumita is the camera-woman. I think we found the Devon/Cornwall film in the box.
Mr BHOSE	Ah...The little cottage with no central heating...sheep walking in our garden..we ate everything with bread because someone had forgotten the rice..

He looks at Mrs Bhose.

Mrs BHOSE	Huh! You and Mohanda played one game of chess, and spent the whole day arguing about it.

Pause.

Mrs SEN	Bhoseda, are you really going to go back? To Calcutta?
Mr BHOSE	We want to.
Mrs SEN	You know, we bought a jommie too in Laketown. By the post office.
Mr BHOSE	Mohanda told me.
Mrs SEN	He bought it in 1985...you see he was going to retire in 1988. The year he passed ...

Skin

Mrs BHOSE [*quickly*] I'm not sure I want to live in Laketown, it's getting so full up..I wanted to go back to Ballygonge, but Bhose won't hear of it.

Mr BHOSE Ballygonge...oof--it's an awful place--what do you say Sumita?

SUMITA [*surprised to be addressed*] What?

Mr BHOSE I said Ballygonge is an awful place, no? Full of poor poets and hopeless artists.

SUMITA I don't know.

Mrs SEN Are you alright dear?

SUMITA Yes I'm fine. I was just thinking.

Mr BHOSE What fine thoughts were in your head?

Pause.

Mrs SEN Sumita, will you get the projector ready?

Sumita goes to the projector. Her pace is determined. Mrs Sen watches her for a moment.

There was no point holding onto it. I realised I was just holding onto a memory.

Mrs BHOSE What?

Mrs SEN I kept our jommie till last month. Then I gave it to my brother.

Mrs BHOSE Kee Bolcho?

Mr BHOSE How come?

Mrs SEN You see, he's only recently married, and his wife is expecting.

Mrs BHOSE But why? Are you not going to...

Mrs SEN Go back? What for? 'A top-up'? [*She smiles*] No, it was Mohanda's dream to live his last years in his beloved Calcutta. I can't chase it.

SUMITA It's ready, shall I turn the lights off?

Mr BHOSE   Aurautidi you shouldn't have given the land away. Maybe in a couple of years you and Sumita...

Mrs SEN   We should chase our dreams, no Bhoseda? Don't take too long, will you.

The lights go off. The projector starts. Images appear on the screen. From the back we see Mr Sen leading a little girl by the hand. Sumita lets out a cry of pain. The projector goes off. A spot goes on Sumita. She's curled up in a little ball on the floor, her thumb in her mouth.

It's OK dear. I'm here.

Mrs Sen moves into the spot and puts her arms around Sumita.

SUMITA   I've let him go. Slip away from me. I didn't want to hurt like you.

MRS SEN   No dear. You have him in you.

SUMITA   He didn't even know me, Ma. He didn't even know Ma. He didn't wait for me to grow up.

MRS SEN   He's knows you now, Sumita. He's seeing everything from above. Come. [*She switches the projector on again*] We'll watch it together. My Sumita.

The spot goes off. The images start again. Countryside. Mrs Sen and Mrs Bhose are opening a picnic. In front of them Mr Bhose throws a ball over the heads off two young children, a girl and a boy, who are running around. Mr Bhose walks towards the camera. The camera changes hands. Mr Sen rushes toward Sumita. Picks her up. She is laughing. Lights down.

GLOSSARY

Lucchi: A ball of dough, flattened and fried into pancakes.
Daal: A lentil sauce.
Cacoo: Uncle.
Puia: A religious festival/ a daily religious prayer.
Jelabees: A rich Indian Sweet.
Jommie: An unbuilt-on plot of land.

Styx and Bones

SAMANTHA DICKINSON

Samantha Dickinson was born in Brisbane, Australia in 1974. She is a university student who has extensive theatre and playwriting experience. She has been a member of various drama groups as actor, playwright, director, sound and lighting technician, and front of house. Several of her plays have been produced in drama festivals and conferences.

CHARACTERS
DOUG, MARLENE, MERV, SALLY, MORTIMER, BARBARA, JAMES

Scene One

The disreputable office of a used car saleyard. Behind a desk sits Marlene. A large banner proclaims 'Preloved Autos - Buy One Today'. Doug is on the phone and Merv is nearby.

DOUG Look, I'm sorry if the car's faulty, but I can't do anything. The business is under new management and I've got no obligation to fix up bomby cars that the last tenant palmed off, okay? Yeah, new management. I didn't sell you that lemon. Doug was the last tenant. When you phoned up and asked to speak to Doug, I said 'yes'. No, I'm Dave. [*Loudly*] Well, I'm sorry, but I'm a bit deaf. Must have misheard you. When did the car yard change management? Only a short time ago, can't remember exactly. You were here yesterday? We only moved in today. I'm sorry madam, but I can't do anything. The tyres fell off when you turned the radio on? Madam, go bother your local mechanic.

He puts the phone down.

MARLENE Dad, you'll get caught one day.

DOUG Survived this long. Don't see why I should get caught now. Especially with you fiddling the books, Merv, me old mate.

MERV I'm not perfect.

DOUG Yeah, but no-one's going to check up on us. We're only a couple of dinky-di Aussies trying to make ends meet.

MARLENE But your ends met and overlapped five times!

DOUG See what your mother's done? Turned you against me.

MARLENE I don't need Mum to tell me. Even I can see you're as crooked as a branch in a magpie's nest.

DOUG She sent me another demand letter today. I'm ignoring it. I mean, I understood her wanting child maintenance when Marlene was a kid. But she's twenty three.

MERV Can we get back to business? Have you come up with a strategy for selling that Morris Minor yet?

Styx and Bones

MARLENE You mean that heap of rust with a bit of car attached to it?

DOUG Don't know why I accepted that trade-in.

MARLENE She batted her false eyelashes at you.

DOUG Pretty little thing.

MARLENE No-one wears such obviously false eyelashes. Not unless they're a call-girl.

DOUG Marlene!

MARLENE It's true.

DOUG Wash your mouth out.

MARLENE Why? I didn't swear.

DOUG Insulting a customer's just as bad.

MARLENE You want a reason? I'll give you a reason. Shit, shit, shit, shit.

MERV Children, please. You're as bad as each other. No-one's going to wash anyone's mouth out. There's a girl looking at the cars! Smile!

DOUG What do you think? Just the basic sell? Yeah.

Doug walks up to Sally.

DOUG Good morning Miss. Doug Hutchinson. Can I help you?

SALLY I'm looking for a car.

DOUG You've come to the right place. What sort of car? A sporty little red car would suit you. Now that I think of it, that P-76 is more your style. And lime green's making a comeback.

SALLY The car's not for me. It's for my Grampy-pie. He wants a new car because his old one's in the dam. All you can see is the bull bar poking out of the water. We don't care what the car looks like. He can't see very well.

DOUG And he's allowed to drive?

SALLY: Not on a real road. But he has a little farm he drives around. Providing someone tells him which way to steer, of course. Poor dear. He used to be a taxi driver and hates to be away on the longest route to the front door. Taxi driving's in his blood.

DOUG: If it doesn't matter about what the car looks like, what about this one? It needs a paint job on the back door, to make it match the other doors. Hey, if you feel really extravagant, you could make the whole car the same colour.

SALLY: What about this one? It looks nice.

Sally goes up to the Morris Minor.

DOUG: It's a great little car.

MARLENE: As long she never opens the bonnet and discovers the monster beneath.

SALLY: Can I test drive it?

DOUG: Why do you need to drive it? Can't you tell by looking at it, it's perfect?

SALLY: It's just that . . .

DOUG: Don't you trust me? I'm hurt. I make the best deal for you, I'm willing to negotiate

SALLY: Negotiate? How much?

DOUG: I'll knock off, ooh, I dunno two hundred.

SALLY: Two hundred off! Three hundred?

DOUG: Two fifty

SALLY: Two seventy-five.

DOUG: You drive a hard bargain. Done.

MARLENE: Dad would have accepted fifty dollars for the thing. The girl's brainless.

MERV: It's his charm. No lady can resist him.

MARLENE: That's what he'd like to think.

DOUG	Here're the keys.
SALLY	Thanks Mr Hutchinson. Bye!

Sally goes. Doug runs into the office.

DOUG	I did it! I sold it! I'm brilliant.
MARLENE	I wonder when she'll bring it back?
DOUG	She won't. This car-yard's perfectly situated on the top of a hill. Even a bomb like that'll start up by the time it's half way down.

Mortimer enters unnoticed with a tote bag that hides a camera.

MARLENE	Yeah. And we have to push them all the way up when they stop at the bottom.
DOUG	Pessimist!
MARLENE	Been reading the dictionary again?
MORTIMER	Excuse me!
DOUG	Not again.
MORTIMER	I am Mortimer.
MORTIMER & DOUG	Investigating journalist for Under The Microscope current affairs show.
DOUG	Yeah, I know. How's your hidden camera?
MORTIMER	What hidden camera?
DOUG	The one you're being very careful to keep pointed in our direction.
MORTIMER	I have been alerted to the fact that you have sold faulty cars on numerous occasions.
DOUG	Moi? Never.
MORTIMER	Sir, a number of my reporters posed as prospective customers and discovered that ...

DOUG	Okay, so a few aren't perfect. But we reduce the price and tell our customers.
MORTIMER	One car had no engine. You made no attempt to point that out.
DOUG	Probably didn't know. Awful pick pockets around here. Steal anything.
MORTIMER	Your aggrieved customers are happy to receive enough money to pay for repairs. If you do that, this will not go to air.
DOUG	How many people do I have to pay?
MORTIMER	I have a list here.
DOUG	Streuth! How am I supposed to pay that much!
MORTIMER	Sell what's left of the business.
DOUG	Never! You're not going to close another of my businesses down.
MORTIMER	If you continue your business I guarantee that TV crews will be checking your cars at least once a week. And next time we will show your shady dealings on TV. Have a nice day.

Mortimer goes.

MARLENE	What are we going to do?
MERV	The best thing is to open up the business under a new name.
DOUG	Don't know if I could go through all that again. The only cars I come by are jinxed.

The phone rings. Doug picks it up.

DOUG	The business is closed. Not you. [*To Marlene*] Your mum. [*To phone*] Lois, I'm not sending money. [*He laughs. To Marlene*] Grandma died. [*To phone*] Why should I pay for her funeral? [*To Marlene*] Your mum says our divorce upset your grandma so much it killed her. [*Back to the phone*] That was fourteen years ago, Lois. Alright, I'll pay half. What do funeral parlours do with the money? Plate bodies in gold? I'll send a cheque. [*He puts down phone*] Don't know where I'll get the money from. Those funeral people charge a fortune.
MERV	They can afford to charge high prices. Everyone dies eventually and something has to be done with the bodies.

Styx and Bones   **69**

MARLENE Yeah. You can't just wack 'em in the wardrobe.

DOUG It's a con job. Bet all those funeral people are rich.

MARLENE Most likely.

DOUG Bet they have big houses and never get bothered by pushy journalists.

MERV Probably.

MARLENE Can't see any of their customers asking for their money back.

MERV Definitely.

All three look at each other and grin.

MARLENE I wonder...

MERV How hard would it be

DOUG To start up our own funeral parlour! First thing we need to decide is what'll make people come to us. A bit cheaper. An extra service.

MARLENE We could rent out the coffins!

DOUG That's it!

MARLENE I was only joking.

DOUG I'm not. We'd only have to buy a few coffins, rent them out for a third of the price of buying one, then reuse them hundreds of times!

DOUG No, Marl. I just smell money.

MARLENE Is it right to profit from corpses? I mean, this is low, even for us!

DOUG They're dead. What do they know? What about a name?

MERV Shouldn't we decide exactly what service we'll provide first?

DOUG A minor detail. A name first. We'll get inspiration from that. How about ...

MERV	A discreet, demure name. With a subtle reference to renting coffins . . .
MARLENE	The sort of name that appeals to the rich.
DOUG	A name that looks nice in fancy writing, with lots of swirls
MERV	Rest In Peace.
DOUG	Too boring. How about Call A Casket?
MARLENE	Hire A Hole?
DOUG	Marl, we're after quality. The One Stop Funeral Shop.
DOUG, MERV & MARLENE	No
MERV	Styx and Bones.
MARLENE	Rent A Box!
DOUG	Marl, you're brilliant!
MARLENE	I was only joking.
DOUG	It's a great name. It states our business. I can see it now in flashing neon lights on the side of the morgue. Rent A Box!

Scene Two

The same office, only the sign has been changed; it now reads 'Rent a Box'. A few objects relating to death are strewn around the room - models of Mary and Jesus, a box of tissues. Doug sits at the desk. Marlene and Merv enter.

MARLENE	What's happened to the outside of the building? I could see it from blocks away. It glows!
MERV	I explained to Marlene it was an undercoat, that the real colour will be up soon but
DOUG	It's the real colour.
MARLENE	You're kidding! It looks like a gigantic bird raided a mulberry tree, then shit all over the building.

DOUG   I know it's not exactly the colour you wanted.

MARLENE   Grey, with a touch of mauve! Are you colour-blind?

DOUG   The painters are coming back next week. Did you get your work done?

MERV   Most of it, yes.

MARLENE   It's not a good idea to start advertising before the business is ready.

DOUG   Won't be long now.

MARLENE   What if someone phones up? We haven't got hearses. And if they want to come here, it still looks like a caryard.

DOUG   Not for long it won't. The bunting's going to be painted black.

MARLENE   Dad!

DOUG   But the sign isn't flashing properly. Bulbs must have broken when they fell off the truck.

MARLENE   What sign?

DOUG   It says Rent A Box. And it's very tasteful.

MARLENE   Flashing lights on a funeral parlour? Merv, how could you let Dad do it? You know?

DOUG   How do you think I paid for your upbringing?

MARLENE   The tooth fairy contributed more to my welfare than you ever did!

DOUG   That's it. It's about time you knew this. I was the tooth fairy.

MERV   I think Marlene was speaking metaphorically.

MARLENE   I don't know why I even work with you.

DOUG   You need the job. That's why.

MARLENE   I could get another one any day.

DOUG	Doing what? I didn't think you could be employed for complaining!
MERV	That's enough boys and girls. You've had your fight for the day. Calm down.
DOUG & MARLENE	No!
MERV	Marlene, tell your father what you did today ... Doug, ask Marlene what she did today.
MERV	Then I'll just have to phone Lois ...
DOUG & MARLENE	No!
MERV	[*replacing the phone.*] Thank you.
DOUG	What did you do?
MARLENE	I put ads in the newspaper.
MERV	Good. Then what did you do?
MARLENE	I stuck posters to noticeboards in old people's homes.
MERV	Doug, please don't make me hand out brochures again. The teenagers thought I was a comedian.
DOUG	Yeah, well my day wasn't perfect either. I phoned my mate Jack to see how the hearse painting was going. He's painted them yellow.
MARLENE	Yellow?
DOUG	Apparently yellow paint's cheaper than black. Don't worry. I persuaded him to paint them black. That, or he'll be taking a ride in one.
MARLENE	Dad, hearses aren't black these days. The latest fashion is silver grey, or mauve, or even white. Didn't you read all that literature I gave you?
DOUG	Course not! Now let's see. We have coffins, we have hearses. We have a driver, an office, ads. After months, the business is almost ready. I've even contacted Soil Incorporated, who own the land we're on. The lawyers can't get in touch with the main partner, but they're sure we'll have no problem renewing the lease.

The phone rings.

MERV I've got it. Hello, Rent A Box. I - I - I - beg your pardon? Just a minute. [*to Doug*] You're better at this.

DOUG [*using his best funeral voice*] Hello, how may I help you? Yes ma'am. Your address? We'll be right over.

[*He replaces the phone.*] We did it! Someone fell for it!

MARLENE But you're booked to speak at the gym!

DOUG Forget about live bodies, we've got a dead one to pick up!

Scene Three

A very bare room. There is an old sofa, coffee table and TV. Barbara enters, followed by Doug and Merv. Merv carries a collapsible stretcher and Doug holds a folder full of brochures.

BARBARA Sit down. This was Great Uncle Henry's room. He didn't bring much with him and I'd be damned if I bought him anything. I knew he didn't have long to go. Would you like a cup of Peruvian tea?

MERV That would be very nice.

DOUG Not for me, thanks. I get vertigo.

Barbara goes.

DOUG What do you think? She looks rich.

MERV But look how she treated Henry. It's ghastly. I wonder where he is? I didn't see him on the way in. Actually, I'm rather nervous. She's our first customer and I don't think she's going to be easy.

DOUG Why don't you put that stretcher down? We don't want to look too much like vultures.

MERV How will you bring up the funeral arrangements?

DOUG Thought I'd ease into it. Same way I did with the cars. Except, where I said cars, engines and speed, I'll now say funerals, coffins and dignity. Nice word, 'dignity'. Looked it up last night.

MERV   I wonder where that body is?

DOUG   Worrying you, is it?

MERV   I've never seen a dead body before. I don't know how I'm going to pick it up.

DOUG   I'll be here to help you.

MERV   What if it's gone into rigor mortis? How do you carry it out gracefully if he died in a peculiar position?

DOUG   We'll send Barbara outside. Tell her it might be upsetting to see him going out the house for the last time.

Barbara enters with a cup of tea and hands it to Merv.

DOUG   Tell me about Great Uncle Henry.

BARBARA   There isn't much to say, really. He arrived two months ago and died today.

DOUG   What did he do for a living before he retired?

BARBARA   A bookie, of all things.

DOUG   [*to Merv*] That means he's probably got a bit stashed away somewhere. She can use that to pay for the funeral.

MERV   'Probably', 'somewhere'. You're clutching at straws.

DOUG   Bookies make money. I should know, I've given them enough.

BARBARA   Unfortunately, he never made any money.

DOUG   Oh.

BARBARA   He was a failure. Never could do anything properly. Not even die.

MERV   Oh?

BARBARA   Terribly inconvenient. Died around noon. I found him when I came home to give him lunch.

DOUG But you only phoned us an hour ago.

BARBARA What else could I do? I thought he might start to smell if I left him until tomorrow.

DOUG About the funeral arrangements.

BARBARA Just the cheapest coffin possible. No service. No-one will come. And cremation, I suppose. You dump the ashes.

DOUG Ma'am, the death of a loved one is very traumatic. You might not care what happens to Great Uncle Henry now. But in a few weeks time, you'll look back at the nasty departure from this world you gave him, and wish you had given him a more dignified and humane exit.

BARBARA Humane? He's dead.

DOUG But his soul lives on. And he'd be mortified by your behaviour.

BARBARA Don't be ridiculous. I don't believe in souls or God.

DOUG If you don't want to do it for Uncle Henry, think about his relatives. The main purpose of a funeral is grief therapy. Someone else's death makes people more aware of their own mortality and they need to be reassured. Great Uncle Henry's relatives need a chance to say good-bye.

BARBARA Alright, I'll have a service. I suppose one or two people might come.

DOUG If you don't think many people will come, we also offer a discrete Rent A Crowd service.

BARBARA No thank you.

DOUG Would you like a minister or celebrant to take the service?

BARBARA Which is cheaper?

DOUG [*quietly to Merv*] The rabbi, celebrant and minister are one person. They cost the same. [*To Barbara*] The minister is cheaper.

BARBARA Him, then.

DOUG And the service will be held in the Chapel of Singing Souls. A lovely place. Now for the funeral wreaths.

BARBARA	I don't want flowers. I get hay fever.
DOUG	We also rent out plastic flowers.
MERV	You'll have to face it, Doug. She doesn't want to part with money.
DOUG	Tell your relatives that they are quite welcome to buy flowers from us if they wish. Now for the coffin.
BARBARA	The cheapest one.
DOUG	Maybe you would like to look at our full colour brochure.
BARBARA	Maybe I wouldn't.
DOUG	We have many beautiful styles.
BARBARA	Look, I have a dinner party to prepare. Perhaps I could call in at your office tomorrow and discuss details?
DOUG	That'll be fine. Where is Uncle Henry?
BARBARA	Oh him. Behind the sofa.

Doug and Merv leap up and move away from the sofa.

MERV	Has he been there all the time?
BARBARA	He's not about to move.
DOUG	Maybe you'd like to leave?
MERV	Thank you.
DOUG	Not you. Barbara.
BARBARA	I'll talk to you later. Bye bye Uncle Henry, next time I see you, you'll be reduced to carbon!

Barbara goes and Merv unfurls the stretcher.

DOUG		I'll grab his head. You hold his feet.
MERV		I'm too old for this. How can you do it?
DOUG		I just pretend it's my ex-wife.

Scene Four

The next day back in the office. Doug, Merv and Marlene are discussing their first client.

DOUG		And then I said, 'Maybe you'd like to leave', And Merv said 'thank you'!

Doug and Marlene both laugh.

MERV		You might think it's funny, but I'd never seen a corpse before. I didn't know what to expect.
DOUG		Just think of them as sheep carcasses.
MARLENE		The customers wouldn't like to hear that.
DOUG		They wouldn't like to know they're stored in a deep freezer either.
MERV		When do we get a proper morgue?
DOUG		As soon as we can afford one.
MARLENE		Dad, someone's parking his bike outside. He's coming this way. He's gorgeous. Wonder if he's got a girlfriend?

James enters, out of breath.

JAMES		Hello. Is this Rent A Box?
DOUG		Yes, we are the friendly staff of Rent-A-Box. How may I help you?
MARLENE		Would you like to sit down? You look exhausted.
JAMES		Thanks. Cycling can be tiring.
MERV		Can't you afford a car?

JAMES   Well, no. But that's not why I ride a bike. It's environmentally sound. Like this place.

MARLENE   Environmentally sound?

DOUG   You know Marlene, because we reuse our coffins, less trees are cut down.

MARLENE   Of course, silly me!

JAMES   A lecturer died and we students decided to pay for her funeral. No relatives, you see.

MARLENE   How sad.

DOUG   Death is indeed sad. We at Rent A Box understand that and will arrange the funeral at a pace to suit you. We won't rush you through this important step in the grieving process just so we can get maximum profit.

MARLENE   [*whispering*] Dad, it sounds like a well rehearsed sales pitch.

DOUG   There's a morgue for the deceased to rest in until the service. Keeping them in one place as long as possible gives continuity between life and death. Here there is love. The city morgue has toe tags. We're also cheaper.

JAMES   We voted on having the funeral in the lecture theatre and we want to talk about her ourselves.

DOUG   Now, about the coffin. We have a large range. Would you like to go and see them now? We even have brochures.

JAMES   Later. Can we arrange the actual funeral now?

DOUG   Of course. Have you thought about viewing the deceased before the funeral? People find it therapeutic to see their loved one before they are finally put to rest.

JAMES   I don't think it's a good idea in this case.

DOUG   Oh?

JAMES   Apparently she looks pretty gruesome.

Styx and Bones

MERV Oh!

JAMES She had a heart attack and fell face down into a dish of indian ink.

MARLENE Oh.

JAMES She'd poured the ink into the dish so she could dip the potatoes in it.

MERV The potatoes?

JAMES Yeah. She was potato printing. She seemed to think indian ink gave a better result. It certainly gave a permanent one. One side of her face is totally black.

DOUG You worrying about a little ink stain? We have cosmeticians who can correct that.

MARLENE We don't!

DOUG We do.

MARLENE Who?

DOUG You.

MARLENE Me? No!

DOUG Yes.

MERV Oh dear.

DOUG Excuse us. Family discussion.

Doug takes Merv and Marlene aside.

MARLENE I'm not painting dead bodies!

DOUG Until we find a real cosmetician, you'll have to.

The three return to James.

Sorry about that. We can cover up that stain for you. Now, if you don't find this too distressing, could you fill this form out? It's about the vital details of the loved one.

MARLENE	Here's a pen.
JAMES	Thank you.
MARLENE	I like your bike. I think it's great that you're so worried about the environment.
JAMES	There's a lot to worry about. Are you doing anything to help save the world?
MARLENE	I don't know much about it.
JAMES	You should come to one of our meetings. We have protests a lot, too. Why don't you come along?
MARLENE	I'd love to!
JAMES	We have a march this arvo to protest against the logging of native trees. We'll be meeting in the city square at four. It'd be great if you could come.
MARLENE	Oh, I will!
MERV	[*looking through window*] Ah Ah.
DOUG	What, Merv?
MARLENE	It's Bimbo. She's back!
MERV	She's walking this way.
DOUG	The car's killed him!

Sally enters.

SALLY	Hello again. I hope I'm not bothering you.
DOUG	Look, I'm really sorry about the whole thing.
SALLY	Oh, thank you.
DOUG	I wish I could help.

Styx and Bones

SALLY — How did you know Grampy-pie died?

DOUG — Where's the car?

SALLY — The bottom of the dam.

MARLENE — So it's true the car killed him!

SALLY — No, Grampy-pie died in his sleep.

DOUG — Then why are you here?

SALLY — To rent a coffin. I saw your display in the supermarket, next to the nut shop. I recognised your faces and suddenly a thought struck me.

MARLENE — A rare occurrence, I'm sure.

SALLY — You knew Grampy-pie. Well, you've seen him. Anyway, I thought it would be nice if Grampy-pie was buried by people he knew.

DOUG — I understand. You were right to come here. Would you like to sit down? Where would you like the funeral to be held?

MERV — Before you discuss details, can I ask a question? Miss, where is your grandfather? He's not in the back of your car, is he? Or behind a sofa?

DOUG — You'll have to excuse Merv. We give him a job because we feel sorry for him. Now, the funeral. We have a very beautiful Chapel of Love and Harmony. Or the Chapel of Singing Souls.

SALLY — What's the Chapel of Love and Harmony like?

DOUG — Soft organ music filters through the flower arrangements like spring sunlight through the leaves of a gumtree. Light cascades through the stained glass windows and casts a golden glow over the Loved One. If you want, we can pump your grandad's favourite aftershave through the air conditioning.

SALLY — That sounds nice. I'll have the funeral there.

DOUG — What flowers would you like for decoration?

SALLY — I don't know what Grampy-pie liked. I like daffodils.

MARLENE	That'd be right. We're in the sub-tropics and she wants daffodils.
DOUG	We can certainly try and get daffodils. Let's look at the coffins. Merv, the pictures. We're proud to say we have a coffin for everyone.
SALLY	How thoughtful. Where do I start? They all look so nice. [*Sally turns to James.*] You look clever. Will you help me?
JAMES	I didn't know your grandfather.
SALLY	No, but if Grampy-pie had known you, he would have liked you. You've got nice shoes.
JAMES	That settles it then.
DOUG	That's the Black Beauty. Lovingly made from varnished teak. With flying angel handles. She's then lined with black velvet that has been painstakingly trimmed with sparkling diamantes.
SALLY	But it wouldn't go with daffodils, would it?
DOUG	No. Now this is the coffin I want to be buried in. The Traditional Teak. Notice the Old Gold handles. The design comes from one of the gold picture frames in the Palace of Versailles [*He pronounces it 'versales'*].
SALLY	Where?
MARLENE	[*pronouncing it correctly*] Versailles. He means Versailles.
SALLY	Where?
MARLENE	In France, where they eat frog legs and snails.
SALLY	Eulch!
JAMES	Don't worry about it. France is a long way away.
SALLY	I don't want Grampy-pie in a coffin with handles designed by people who eat frogs!
DOUG	Do you want to look at the next model?

Styx and Bones

SALLY: I like it. It's bright.

MARLENE: Unlike you.

DOUG: Marl! Make another comment like that and you'll be in the showroom polishing coffins. [*To Sally.*] Yes, it's a nice piece of work. We call it the Blue Moon. It's one of our even more environmentally friendly coffins.

JAMES: Environmentally friendly?

DOUG: Yes. You see, The Blue Moon, and a couple of other models, are made out of almond shells. They um ... Merv, you explain.

MERV: What happens is Almond shells are pulverised and mixed with something, then it's poured into a mould. But they are so clever the almond shell coffin looks as good as wood.

SALLY: I saw your ad next to a nut shop. It's fate!

MERV: But the coffins aren't edible.

DOUG: Thank you Merv. We have another almond shell coffin somewhere. Ah! The Pink'n'Pretty.

SALLY: It's pink! [*To James*] I like it. Do you? By the way, I'm Sally.

JAMES: I'm James. How do you do?

SALLY: Good. How are you?

JAMES: Great.

SALLY: Well, I'm fine except that my grandfather died.

JAMES: I'm sorry. My lecturer died. I'm sure losing a relative is worse than losing a teacher.

SALLY: What if they're both?

JAMES: I suppose you're doubly sad!

SALLY: That would be awful.

DOUG: Excuse me. Pink'n'Pretty?

SALLY: I'm sorry. Please tell me about it.

DOUG: Besides being made of almond shells, Pink'n'Pretty is lined with pink satin and trimmed with velvet bows and lace. The deceased rests their head on a heart-shaped pink velvet cushion.

SALLY: I can imagine myself lying in it. But is it right for Grampy pie?

JAMES: How about you toss out the coffins you don't like, then whittle down the pile and see if you end up with the pink one?

SALLY: You're so clever. I knew you were.

She sorts the coffins into two piles.

SALLY: James, what do you think of this one?

JAMES: The lid made out of saloon doors is certainly original. But I think it's more suited to my inebriated lecturer.

DOUG: Does this mean you've decided on a coffin?

JAMES: Not yet, but I'll keep the Western Wonder in mind.

SALLY: I wish you had one in the shape of a taxi. Only two left. Pink'n'Pretty and Pharaoh's Gold. I'll choose Pink'n'Pretty. Gosh, look at the time! Do you mind if we do the rest of the arrangements later? I've got a hair appointment. How about I come back afterwards?

DOUG: Great.

JAMES: Do you mind if I do the same? I've a tute.

DOUG: Sure. See you both soon.

SALLY: Do you need a lift, James?

JAMES: Why not? It saves me pedalling.

SALLY See you soon. Bye!

Sally and James go.

MARLENE I thought he was concerned about the environment. Just because she's pretty. Dad, stop them both! Yell at them before they get away!

DOUG Marl, don't you think you're taking this jealousy thing a bit far?

MARLENE Jealous? Dad! We've got to get death certificates off them!

DOUG Death certificates?

MARLENE Yeah. You need one from a doctor before you can bury a person. You must have got one when you picked up that other man's body. It's illegal not to.

Doug and Merv look at each other in horror.

DOUG & MERV A death certificate!!

Scene Five

The Rent a Box office. Marlene is bashing at the computer keys with an opened can of condensed milk beside her. Every so often she eats a spoonful of it. Sally and James are on the other side of the office, waiting to see Doug.

SALLY I've never been almost arrested before. I hope those trees appreciate that.

JAMES I have. I'm a uni student.

SALLY I wish I was clever enough to go to uni. What do you study?

JAMES I've studied biology, French, geography. You name it, I've studied it. Although, I've never actually finished a course. I keep transferring.

Merv enters reading a newspaper.

MERV Good morning Marl.

MARLENE Sally and James are here. They want to see Dad.

MERV   Why?

MARLENE   Who cares? Is that today's paper? Can I borrow it for a sec? Taurus. 'Stay in bed.'

SALLY   I miss Grampy-pie. But it helps to think of how happy he is up there in Heaven. He can see now and he drives all around the clouds.

JAMES   Your Heaven sounds nice.

SALLY   It's not my Heaven. Anyone can get in. As long as they've been good. When I go to Heaven, I'll play the harp.

MERV   How did the protest go last night?

MARLENE   I don't care if every bloody tree in every bloody forest is cut down by every bloody logger in Australia. In fact, I hope they are.

MERV   It didn't go well, then?

MARLENE   I should have realised it was going all wrong when James invited Sally in the first place. It was disgusting. They were making googly-eyes at each other all through the protest. It was gross.

SALLY   One thing worries me. So many people have died, wouldn't it be a bit crowded up there?

JAMES   Maybe there's a waiting list.

SALLY   That's not fair. How do you decide who's at the front of the queue? How long they've been waiting or how good they've been? And why don't you bump into all the souls when you're in a plane?

JAMES   Maybe they move out of the way. Maybe God warns them. Do you want to come to my place for dinner?

SALLY   I'd like that.

MARLENE   They're supposed to be mourning. What does he see in her?

Doug enters.

DOUG   I hope you're not talking about a customer Marl. Eating condensed milk? You'll get spots.

MARLENE   Don't care.

Sally and James continue googlying.

DOUG   Can we help you?

JAMES   Oh, sorry. We were wondering if it's too late to change the funeral arrangements.

SALLY   You see, we get on so well, we've decided to hold a double funeral.

JAMES   For my lecturer and her Grampy-pie.

DOUG   Well, the funerals are tomorrow and we have organised everything.

JAMES   We understand that it would be difficult.

SALLY   So we're willing to pay extra.

DOUG   We can work something out.

SALLY   We thought we could divide the Chapel of Love and Harmony into two. James and his friends sit on one side and mine sit on the other.

JAMES   The coffins can lie side by side up the front during the service.

SALLY   And both coffins can be cremated together.

MARLENE   True love.

SALLY   Can you do it?

DOUG   No problems. We'll see you before the funeral.

SALLY   Thank you. Bye.

James and Sally leave.

MARLENE   Bimbo. Bitch. Man stealer. I hate you!

Marlene throws a tissue box at the door. Mortimer enters and catches the box.

MARLENE It wasn't aimed at you. Honest. I hope it didn't damage your camera.

MORTIMER I don't have a camera.

MARLENE I knew I should have stayed in bed.

Marlene eats condensed milk.

MORTIMER I'm making an unofficial visit to check up on the business.

DOUG Everything's fine. No complaints.

MORTIMER I held a brief inspection of the premises and everything seems to be in order. Now that's is over, on to pleasure. [*He gets three pieces of paper out of his bag.*] I used an identikit to generate likenesses of you all. I enjoy creating pictures of my friends and associates in my spare time.

MARLENE What fun.

MORTIMER It's difficult to create exact likenesses of people on one of these kits. There's a new computer identikit I'd like.

MARLENE Great. I bet you memorise plane schedules too.

DOUG Marl! Mort, come see our coffin room. Bring your camera. You might find something dodgy.

Doug and Mortimer go out.

MERV You shouldn't talk like that to journalists. You never know what they may do.

MARLENE I don't care.

MERV This James thing is upsetting you, isn't it?

MARLENE I didn't even know Sally was coming. She just turned up. James said, "I asked Sally to come. You don't mind, do you?" What could I say? I'm becoming a nun. Why do we fall for the wrong people?

MERV Human nature, I suppose.

MARLENE Maybe James'll drop Sally. Maybe I could help speed up the process.

Doug and Mortimer enter.

DOUG His beeper went off. Now he needs our phone.

MORTIMER [*using the phone*] Hello June, my beeper went off. I'm being sent where? Antarctica? On orders from Murdoch? What did I do wrong? It was only a joke. Where's his sense of humour? Hello? [*He puts down the phone*] I've been relocated. I won't be able to close down any more of your businesses.

DOUG What a shame.

Mortimer begins to leave.

MARLENE Hey, Morty! Would you like some condensed milk? [*Mortimer goes.*] Always works for me.

DOUG Come on Merv, let's grab some fish'n'chips and celebrate. No more Mort, can you believe it?

Doug and Merv go.

MARLENE One problem gone. Now for Sally. Swap the funerals. She's out, I'm in.

Marlene swaps the funeral arrangements on the computer.

Scene Six

The office on the day of the funerals arranged by Barbara, Sally and James. Marlene is happy as she works. Merv and Doug enter.

DOUG Feeling better today Marl? No condensed milk?

MARLENE No condensed milk.

MERV You haven't done anything, have you Marlene?

MARLENE Moi?

Barbara storms in.

BARBARA   Pink! The whole chapel is pink! It looks like an Arabian harem! I hate pink!

DOUG   You didn't ask for pink?

BARBARA   No, you fool.

DOUG   I don't know how it could have happened. Marl, show me the bookings. I'm sorry, but it says you ordered a pink funeral.

BARBARA   I didn't! It looks very expensive and I didn't order it.

MERV   I'm sure there's been a simple mistake. If you just calm down, we can correct it.

DOUG   I don't know how it could have happened. Maybe the computer is mucking up.

BARBARA   Where's my funeral?

DOUG   If you haven't got it, then it must be.

Sally enters in tears. James enters, trying to comfort her.

SALLY   It's horrible. Everything's black! The coffin's a plain wooden box!

DOUG   There's been a terrible mix up. If you'll just wait a while, I'll sort it all out. This is a very grave matter and I'll do everything I can.

James finds the pun funny and laughs.

MARLENE   We're such a young business, we only have a skeleton staff.

James laughs again, and laughs at every joke Marlene makes. Sally cries even more.

JAMES   I'm sorry, Sally. I didn't mean to laugh.

MARLENE   We work to a very tight deadline and sometimes things go wrong.

SALLY   My poor Grampy-pie! How can you laugh, James?

JAMES   I'm sorry. But you have to admit she's good.

DOUG   I promise. No more references to death.

Styx and Bones

MARLENE	I'd kill for an apple right now.
SALLY	You laugh once more James and I'll split the funeral!
DOUG	Marlene!
MARLENE	I almost bought some this morning. But a guy got to them first. It's the quick or the dead at sales.
SALLY	That's it! Get my Grampy-pie away from him!
DOUG	Marlene, shut up.
MARLENE	Fine, from now on, any funeral references are dead and buried.
DOUG	Marlene. I'll speak to you later! Sally, you come with me and we'll sort your funeral out. Come on Merv, I'll need help.

Doug, Merv and Sally leave.

JAMES	That really was an awful thing to do to her.
MARLENE	I know. But I enjoyed it.
JAMES	Can I be equally insensitive and ask you out after the funeral?
MARLENE	I should say no. In fact, I will say no.
JAMES	What? I thought you wanted me to ask you out!
MARLENE	I did. I just have no intention of making it easy for you. Go on, crawl.
JAMES	Please, Marlene. Please come and have coffee with me.
BARBARA	And what about my funeral service? Why are they seeing to that girl first?
MARLENE	She ordered the more expensive funeral. You'll have to leave now Madam. I have to practise 'Amazing Grace' on the organ.
BARBARA	I will not. I'll stay here until my funeral is black again. Anyway, why should I? I won't steal anything.
MARLENE	I'm not worried about that. I'm scared you'll frighten the customers away. Come on, James. Crawl a bit more!

JAMES		Has anyone ever told you how sexy assertive women are?

Marlene and James leave.

BARBARA		Fancy giving me a pink funeral.
VOICE		I like pink!
BARBARA		Who said that? Where are you?
VOICE		I said that! And I'm everywhere.
BARBARA		Whoever you are, I don't like tricks. Are you one of my students?
VOICE		A student? No, I'm your Great Uncle Henry.
BARBARA		You can't be Great Uncle Henry. He's dead.
VOICE		I know I'm dead. But now I'm back. To visit you.
BARBARA		If you're really Great Uncle Henry, tell me something only you would know.
VOICE		Simple. I know where your birthmark is. I remember seeing it for the first time when you were about four months old. It's right--
BARBARA		Alright, you don't have to tell the world. Why are you here?
VOICE		I want a better funeral. I don't like black.
BARBARA		Too late. I've already paid for your funeral.
VOICE		[*booms*] Change it!
BARBARA		Alright! I will! As soon as they get back.
VOICE		I want music, and singing, and flowers, and beautiful hymns. Do you understand?
BARBARA		Yes! Just don't shout at me.
VOICE		By the way, if you don't do as I ask, I'll start wearing chains and haunt your house! Good bye, Barbara!

BARBARA Wait!

VOICE [*fading away*] Don't forget! A nice funeral!

Doug, Merv and Marlene enter.

DOUG We've got your funeral out of the Chapel of Love and Harmony and we're transferring it across to the Singing Souls right now.

BARBARA Stop! I've changed my mind. I want the most expensive funeral you've got. And he wants music. What else? A choir. Everything.

DOUG [*shouting out the window*] Stop moving that black stuff! She wants the deluxe model! Stop staring, do it!

BARBARA I'm eternally grateful for this.

Barbara goes.

MERV What luck! Wonder what changed her mind?

DOUG Who cares! It means more money!

MARLENE Yeah!

Doug, Merv and Marlene laugh and cheer. The phone rings.

DOUG Hello, Rent a Box, can I help you? What do you want, Lois? ... The land lease contract? ... The Soil Company's what? [*He puts down the phone*] Did either of you realise soil is an anagram of Lois?

THE END

Windows

Richard Hannay

Richard Hannay was born in Queensland in 1976. In 1992 his first play won a prize in the QATIS State Literary Competition and has been produced in the North Queensland Drama Festival. He is a student at James Cook University in Townsville studying English and Performance Writing.

Windows

CHARACTERS

FEMALE/EMMA
MALE
VOICE, *Offstage news presenter*
VELOURIA FRANCIS, *Adult Aboriginal woman*
POD GREENE, *Adult Aboriginal man*
HARRY ROSWELL, *Adult white man*
EMMA ROSWELL, *Adult white woman*

F   Where are my legs?

M   Lie down.

F   I can't feel my legs!

M   Please, don't try to sit up.

F   Where are they? Let me see them.

M   Trust me, they are in one piece.

F   They don't feel that way.

M   How do they feel now?

F   It's hard to say.

M   Shut your eyes.

F   My head hurts.

M   Don't fight it.

F   Give me something for my headache, please!

M   Calm yourself, it will pass. You are going to be O.K.

F   Don't go!

_____	M	You need rest.
_____	F	There is something wet in this bed!
_____	M	Moving will only spread the pain.
_____	F	I want to see someone.
_____	M	Who?
_____	F	My mother.
_____	M	She will be here when you wake up.
_____	F	I need to see her.
_____	M	Visiting hours are over.
_____	F	I can't sleep. Don't go yet!
_____	M	What is it?
_____	F	I want the doctor to look at my legs.
_____	M	Go to sleep.
_____	F	No, please! Don't turn off the light! Leave the light on!

The stage lights up and reveals two figures standing opposite each other at either side of the stage. On the left, struggling against heavy chains is a young man called Pod Greene. Between gasps, he occasionally calls to Velouria Francis, a middle-aged woman who is also in chains on the right of the stage.

_____	VELOURIA	Let me out!
_____	POD	Don't waste your time.
_____	VELOURIA	I have done nothing!
_____	POD	Don't waste your time!
_____	VELOURIA	These chains, they might come loose. Pull hard against the wall. Help me!

POD		They can't hear you.
VELOURIA		These walls are not that thick. [*To the distance*] I have not done a thing!
POD		They won't be listening. Please, stop your screaming.
VELOURIA		Pull on your chains. You're strong... you could break them.
POD		My arms will break before these chains. I can't even get comfortable.
VELOURIA		Help me out of here! Look at me! I'm chained to a wall. It's so damn dark, I can't tell if my hands are bleeding.
POD		Please --
VELOURIA		If this is some sick joke... Pod, is that light coming through the floor?
POD		Wait.
VELOURIA		Is that light? Take a look! Don't fool around.
POD		Just shut up.
VELOURIA		Don't *stuff* me around, Pod. Don't ignore me, you little bastard. You have to help me get out of here. Snap out of it! [*Pod fights against the chains*] Help.

The lights fade out and then return to reveal a figure lying on a bed in tahe centre of the stage. Emma Roswell lies motionless under the sheets. A news broadcast Voice coming from offstage can slowly be heard getting louder.

VOICE		...she is in stable condition, but doctors fear she may lose the use of her body from the waist down, due to the massive injuries suffered in the fall. In Perth today, an Aboriginal couple have been held in custody, and are expected to be charged with murder following an investigation into the brutal attack.

As the voice continues, Emma stirs and slowly tries to make her way from the bed to the darkness on the left of the stage. She drags herself along the floor with great difficulty.

VOICE		Senior police investigators said that before the unprovoked attack, the victim and the two charged had been drinking. Police sources also indicated that the incident was drug-related, but stressed that the victim was not part of the drug scene. The Opposition spokesman for Law & Order today joined police, the

victims family and supporters in condemning the attackers and have called for maximum punishment. The victim's parents, in an emotional interview on national television, said the death penalty would hardly be compensation for the pain and suffering of their daughter in her future life as a paraplegic.

As the voice fades out, Emma screams and remains pinned to the floor. Harry Babel soon enters and rushes to find Emma on the floor. Harry is dressed in a nondescript uniform, and has an almost military walk.

HARRY What on earth have you done? Emma, lift your head.

EMMA Help me.

HARRY How did you get over here?

EMMA Please.

HARRY Have you hurt yourself? Let me see your legs. [*Harry examines her*] I can't imagine that there would be too much pain. Please, lift your head.

EMMA Don't touch me, Harry. Let me rest.

HARRY Are you feeling dizzy? Have you dirtied yourself again [*Harry takes her hand*] Are the migraines returning?

EMMA Let me rest.

HARRY Where were you trying to go? Emma, let me help.

EMMA To the window. I needed some fresh air.

HARRY The windows are barred.

EMMA And some sunlight. I needed to warm myself.

HARRY It's nearly midnight.

EMMA I find it hard to tell the time of day. Please don't do this, Harry.

HARRY I think you may have had another bad dream. We're going to cut down the medication a little.

EMMA	No, the dreams are fine. It's when I'm awake...
HARRY	Yes?
EMMA	It doesn't matter.
HARRY	Tell me.
EMMA	Please, no.
HARRY	Emma...
EMMA	Go away.
HARRY	I suppose you want a hand to get back into bed?
EMMA	I need a hand, not want one. Just pass me a pillow, I'd like to rest here.
HARRY	Don't be foolish. The floor is a mess; it's unhealthy and you could freeze to death.
EMMA	Just a pillow Harry.
HARRY	[*Harry places a pillow under Emma's head*] I'll be back to check on you.
EMMA	I won't be awake. I'll be dreaming.

The lights fade and then return to focus on Pod and Velouria, who still remain chained to the walls facing each other.

VELOURIA	Pod, wake up. [*Pod hangs from his chains and does not move*] Pod. I can smell food, wake up! [*Pod's head lifts*].
POD	What?
VELOURIA	I can smell food. [*Pod raises his head and sniffs the air.*] It smells like bread.
POD	I can't smell a thing.
VELOURIA	Somebody is cooking. This means its morning, it might be our breakfast, Pod!

POD   What did we agree about food fantasies?

VELOURIA But this...

POD   Just ignore it, Velouria. The hunger will go away.

VELOURIA But how often do they cook fresh food in the morning? Smell it!

POD   It isn't morning. The sun set about an hour ago.

VELOURIA Don't spoil this for me.

POD   Listen, Velouria.

VELOURIA Why try so hard to make this worse?

POD   Listen for the heaters. They turn off after midnight.

VELOURIA I don't want to know. [*Velouria twists uncomfortably.*] I can never sleep in these chains.

POD   Just let yourself hang.

VELOURIA It hurts my hands.

POD   They go numb. Your knuckles will get used to it.

VELOURIA No way.

POD   Just watch me. [*Pod hangs from the wall by the chains.*] See? My hands are nearly used to it.

VELOURIA [*Velouria tries to hang but fails.*] I hope I never get used to doing this.

POD   I need to sleep.

VELOURIA Really? Big day ahead tomorrow, Pod? Planned a bit of excitement for yourself? Save a bit of energy?

POD   Amuse yourself then bitch. [*Pod tries to get comfortable.*] I want to be in one piece when we leave.

VELOURIA	Oh, and we're leaving are we? How nice!
POD	Yes... Eventually.
VELOURIA	Who is fantasising now? [*Pod fights again in his chains.*] Be careful, Pod. You might lose it before that day comes. We both might.

The lights on the two figures fade. Gradually the light returns to focus on Emma, who stands alone in the centre of the stage. The news broadcast Voice slowly returns and breaks the silence. Emma does not move while the voice speaks.

VOICE	There were emotional scenes in the Supreme Court today when Judge Killroy sentenced two Aborigines to ten years jail with hard labour for an attack on a woman, which left her crippled for life. Friends and supporters were cleared from the court when they reacted angrily to what they claimed was too lenient a sentence for a crime which had shocked the state. The court heard that the victim was thrown from her fourth floor unit in a totally unprovoked attack.
EMMA	[*As the Voice stops, Emma walks slowly downstage*] I was nearly five years old. My mum had made me put my hair in piggy-tails, so that I would look pretty, but I knew she was only trying to hide the wildness in me. Making me look human. I would hold her hand through the school gate. Smile as she waved through the glass. But when she turned her sad head, I would shake the piggy-tales out and laugh as my pounding feet beat a steady rhythm on the hot dirt. But I was not a bad girl. Nobody ever said that I was bad. But even I could tell there was something inside me I could not control. Something scary. My friends would run their fingers through my hair. We would spit from the heights of the slippery-slide onto the dirty boys below. But still I could not help but want to kill the girl with the red hair. I could feel my mother's hand against my cheek. I could see my mother combing the girl's long red hair. It made me kick her in the back and watch her somersault onto the gravel. It made me stare while the others screamed as the blood poured from every part of her body. Even as the tears that eventually dripped from my face fell between the steel bars on the slide, I failed to feel the wildness flee from my soul. This was the first time I had cried properly. The first time tears had stained my face for somebody else's pain. It was the first time that guilt had possessed my body and exiled my spirit. But it was not the last. [*Emma slowly sits and then lies on the stage*] Now I can only run wild in my dreams.

The light fades from Emma and returns onto Pod and Velouria.

POD		I would kill for a chance to stretch my legs. Just five minutes away from these chains.
VELOURIA		And this cell.
POD		At least we got fed today.
VELOURIA		At least. [*POD starts coughing*] Don't start that crap again. Listen to me! You'll drive me crazy.
POD		I can't help it.
VELOURIA		Of course you can. You don't see me coughing, do you? Well?
POD		You don't have a fever.
VELOURIA		You don't know that!
POD		Do me a favour and leave me alone. Try and have just a little respect for how I feel.
VELOURIA		I hope the food gets here soon [*POD coughs again*] Maybe I should have your share?
POD		Thanks, but no thanks.
VELOURIA		It's not good to eat when you feel crook...
POD		Knock it off. I'd like to think I could trust you a bit more.
VELOURIA		How long has it been?
POD		How long has what been?
VELOURIA		How long have we been here?
POD		I have no idea.
VELOURIA		Just make an estimate.
POD		I don't know.

VELOURIA   When we get out, I'm going to get in my car and drive around the country.

POD   Can I come?

VELOURIA   I thought you'd be sick of me by now?

POD   Maybe the car is gone.

VELOURIA   I hope I can still drive. Are you sick of me yet? Pod?

Pod does not answer, but hangs his head as the lights fade. The light focuses on centre stage, where Emma sits in a wheelchair facing the audience.

EMMA   Harry. [*She does not move as she calls.*] Harry.

Harry enters.

HARRY   Good morning.

EMMA   Harry, I want you to open the window for me.

HARRY   Is that a good idea?

EMMA   I want you to open the window so I can see outside for a change.

HARRY   Take my word for it, [*he turns and begins making the bed*] it's not much nicer outside than in.

EMMA   Then I want you to tell everyone what we have done.

HARRY   And what have we done? [*He continues making the bed.*]

EMMA   I want to tell the truth, [*Harry stops.*] and I want the two who are in jail to be let out.

HARRY   Emma, this is insane.

EMMA   We lied.

HARRY   What?

EMMA   I can't keep lying like this.

HARRY   Keep your bloody voice down.

EMMA   I just want the two to go free.

HARRY   Don't be stupid.

EMMA   I jumped Harry. It was four floors up and I went through the window.

HARRY   You were pushed.

EMMA   You saw me jump.

HARRY   You were pushed.

EMMA   Two people are rotting in gaol because I lied. And you helped me.

HARRY   The police knew you were pushed.

EMMA   They didn't care.

HARRY   The two were found guilty.

EMMA   Everybody helped me lie and somebody had to pay.

HARRY   Why the hell are you doing this after all these years?

EMMA   I wanted to die and I was too ashamed.

HARRY   You need a shot. I'll get the nurse.

EMMA   I tried to die, only I killed two others. I wanted to be rid of everything. To be happy.

HARRY   Look at me.

EMMA   Open the window, Harry.

HARRY   Don't do this to me.

EMMA   Open the window, then tell the truth.

HARRY   I will burn for this. I've been so good to you. I love you.

EMMA   The truth, Harry.

The light fades. Again the news broadcast Voice breaks the silence.

VOICE   The State's judicial and police systems were shaken today when a woman admitted she had attempted suicide six years ago, and had not been attacked by two Aboriginals now serving ten years in gaol for her assault. In a letter to the State Minister for Justice, the woman, who is a paraplegic, said her injuries had been self-inflicted when she jumped from her fourth floor unit in 1988.

The light returns. Pod and Velouria stand in position. Harry is facing the audience, and Emma sits in her wheelchair with her back to the audience. Harry walks forward.

HARRY   Lying is an easy thing. Only the truth can be dangerous. When guilt sits in someone's soul, and eats at the very core of their being, and when they slash their wrists, they always bleed the truth. But these two...[*Harry points to Pod and Velouria*]...they could have died the minute they were thrown in here. Even freedom couldn't save them. I could blame myself, but I won't take the fall for her again. [*The light focuses on Emma.*] I can't and won't let this happen.

EMMA   Leave the window open, Harry. [*Harry knocks the wheelchair and Emma falls onto the ground*] Harry, help, don't leave me. [*Harry turns and leaves*] Please don't leave me.

When Emma stops screaming the lights fade and the news broadcast Voice begins.

VOICE   ...she had blamed the two Aborigines out of guilt, and now claims she was mentally unstable at the time. Meanwhile, the State Police Union has warned of industrial action if the minister presses for a judicial inquiry into how the police obtained confessions from the two innocent Aborigines.

THE END

Cho Doi (Market of Lives)

LE QUY DUONG

Le Quy Duong was born in Vietnam in 1968 and is a graduate of the University of Theatre and Film in Hanoi. He has won gold medals for three of his plays at festivals in Vietnam and has written reviews for theatre magazines and newspapers. He is a member of the Hanoi Arts Council and the Playwrights' Centre and currently works for the Ministry of Culture in Hanoi.

TRANSLATION BY LE ANH LINH
TRANSLATION EDITED BY ELIANE ANH-XUAN MOREL AND ANDREW WORSSAM

For my mother, and all my good friends.

Market of Lives

CHARACTERS

TRUNG, *Blind war-veteran who sells Dong Ho pictures (Vietnamese traditional pictures) at the markets.*
TRAN CONG, *Cadre of the city*
PHUONG, *Tran Cong's wife*
SONG ANH, *Tran Cong and Phuong's daughter, a student at the teacher's training college*
TU DU, *Song Anh's boyfriend, also a student at the teacher's training college*
THANH, *An invalid war-veteran*
LE, *Thanh's girlfriend, a cleaner in the market*
TO, *Market Manager*
MRS NGA, *Seller of herbal medicines in the markets*
TOM, *Mrs Nga's son, newpaper-seller*
THIET, *Tran Cong's secretary*

Scene One

A shabby and muddy market. Very early morning. Everything seems to be still sleeping. Mrs. Nga is taking out the winnowing basket of cigarettes. Mr Trung is making traditional dong ho pictures with his sense of touch. Thanh is staggering about, as if still asleep. In the distance, Le is sweeping. Suddenly, some gamblers can be heard quarrelling loudly.

TO [*Whistling as he enters the market*] Who? Who? Who's gambling so early in the morning? Who's picking a fight? Why are you making the market so noisy?

GAMBLERS Good Morning! This is only a friendly meeting. We've only come down here to get meat for our children, that's all.

TO [*smiling*] Oh! I see! But you know you must be pleasant to each other when you get together, be friendly

GAMBLERS ... Helping and sharing with each other. Good morning Mr To. Ha ha ha ha!

TO That is right. Remember this is a market.

NGA It must have order, discipline and regulations.

TO Don't interrupt me! You've just been let into the market. If you keep interrupting me like that you'll have to go somewhere else to earn your living. Understand?

Enter Trung.

LE   What are you doing here so early today?

TRUNG   I've been hearing happy sounds coming from the market. I've been listening to To singing as happily as a bird, not grumbling, like he usually does.

TO   You're blind, it makes your ears very sensitive. Your hearing's so good you can hear the very market breathing.

TRUNG   I was born here, grew up here. You know, there used to be a river here. Gradually, the river silted up and eventually became the village and the markets. [*to To*] So, tell us, what makes you so happy? Tell everybody, please!

TO   Listen, listen everybody! Listen carefully! Today, everyone must be well-dressed.

GAMBLER 1   My shirt's ok, but my trousers have some patches

GAMBLER 2   My trouser's don't have any patches but my shirt's torn

TO   Hmm! You have to know how to show off the good, and hide the bad! Two of you exchange clothes. The one with the good shirt sits in front. The one with the patched trousers stands behind. Is that clear?

GAMBLERS   Yes, that's clear.

TO   Alright, off you go! Do what I've told you!

TRUNG   What are you hiding, Mr To?

TO   Today there is a cadre coming to visit the market. It'll be wonderful!

NGA   Oh my God! Another cadre! What'll they do this time? Increase our taxes again, or inspect our trade licences, or

TO   No, no, something much more significant. He's coming here to conduct a survey for the preparation of a new market!

TRUNG   You mean a new market will replace the old one?

Market of Lives

TO   Yes, that's right! This muddy, shabby old market will be flattened and a nice new one will be built.

NGA   Bigger and more beautiful. Just like his words

TO   You're interrupting me again! Just like whose words?

NGA   Uncle Ho! Uncle Ho Chi Minh's words And it's what we've always wanted.

LE   Dear Mr To! That's great news! A new market! But is it really true?

TO   Yes, this time it's true. So, let's get motivated. We must implement a plan of action. Now, let's get down to details... Mrs Nga and the herbalists will take the rubbish from the sewers on the left. Mr Xom and the [*dog-meat*] butchers will clear the sewers on the right. Miss Le and the grocers and cyclo drivers will do the sewers out the back. My son will direct the group of rice sellers to clear the drains in the front. Any objections?

EVERYONE   Let's do it, let's go!

TRUNG   What! Sewers on all four sides! So many years have gone by and we're still surrounded by sewerage?

TO   Nothing changes. Your eyes are damaged, you can't see the filth, so you believe that everything around us is clean.

NGA   Oh, Mr Trung! Don't be sad, it won't do you any good.

THANH   [*getting up with his guitar and singing*] 'ah my Country, my country, my country...'

LE   [*rushing to hold Thanh*] Thanh! Thanh! Here I am! Don't do that! Everyone's preparing to build a new market!

THANH   La la la la la la! Constructions in yellow sunlight, constructions nice with lots of hope...la la la

TO   Oh my God! The madman! How can we make him come to his senses?

THANH   [*singing*] 'One lives with the other for love, For today, for tomorrow, for many following generations'.

NGA	What a pity. He's losing himself again. Le! Here, take some herbal leaves for him to chew, see if that'll do him any good.
TRUNG	He may well be the happiest person in the market. He sounds very happy when he's singing.
LE	Oh Trung! What am I to do with him now?
TRUNG	Let him sing. He's like me. We'd rather see nothing and understand nothing, wouldn't we Mr Thanh?
LE	No! Mr Trung, Mr To, Mrs Nga, please, try to explain to him what's happening. The song's he's singing are pointless. Thanh! You have to live in reality even if it's sad. You can't live in your dreams! Thanh ...
THANH	'For today, for tomorrow, for many generations'.
TO	Thanh! Do you recognise me? It's me, To!
THANH	Stand uprightly! Artist Thanh greets artist Vo Van To.
LE	[*crying*] Oh Thanh!
THANH	[*slapping Le's cheek*] 'Do you still remember the sad city'. I'd like to greet great artist Le.
TO	What a terrible business! Terrible business! When the cadre comes, what will he think of us if he sees Thanh carrying on like this? Whoever Thanh meets, he calls, 'artist'.
THANH	When thinking of a life, I remember a forest. When thinking of a forest, I suddenly remember a lot of other people...
TO	Oh Thanh! Please, please, I beg of you, be quiet. The cadre is coming!

Thanh continues singing then falls asleep.

TO	Yes, yes, that's right, keep sleeping. Have a good nap. Sleep all day long if you like. When there's a new market you'll be able to sing to your heart's content.
LE	Sleep my darling! Tomorrow I'll take you to hospital. The people in the market have collected some money for you to go there again.

Market of Lives 111

NGA — Oh my God! Miss Le, Mr Trung is drawing a picture of you! Mr Trung, Mr Trung! How can you do that? How do you do it?

TRUNG — I hear the voice and know what the person looks like! Le's voice, listen, it's warm, just like the earth....Mr To! Don't let anyone walk on this picture I've drawn of Le!

TO — You know, rain will come and the water will wash it away. Say, Trung, were you ever a painter?

TRUNG — Long ago. A very long time ago. Perhaps if the war hadn't deprived me of my vision.

TO — You're a war-invalid. Why don't you live in the war-invalid's camp? How can you improve your life painting pictures in this market?

TRUNG — You don't understand.

Someone laughs loudly outside.

TO — Shut up! It's going to be difficult to get him to sleep.

TRUNG — Who is it? His laughter is almost inhuman.

TO — He's a debt collector, and not afraid of using violence to get money out of people. His name's Phi Bba Phay. [*To Ba Phay*] Alright! I don't care whether you laugh or not now! But when the cadre comes, I don't want to hear you laughing like this. If you do, don't blame me for the consequences!

Tran Cong, Song Anh and Thiet enter the market, smiling.

TRAN CONG — Here I am.

TO — Oh, what a surprise! Mr Cong! Mr Thiet! And your daughter! When did you arrive? I'll prepare something to--

TRAN CONG — No, no ceremonies, please. Consider me like everyone else. Treat me as if I was an ordinary person.

TO — I would like to introduce Mr Tran Cong to you all. A summary of his achievements has been distributed to everyone in the market, so they'll know who to vote for in the next People's Committee election. He will manage the construction of the new market. Everybody! Bravo!

TRAN CONG	Good morning everyone!
TRUNG	[*Speaking to himself*] That voice, that voice is so familiar. Could it be him? Could it?
NGA	[*Surprised*] Excuse me! Are you Mr Cong?
TRAN CONG	What? What are you saying?
NGA	Were you in Truong Son during the war? I'm not sure, but are you...?
TRAN CONG	Yes, I was fighting in Truong Son. Were you?
NGA	No, I must be mistaken.
TO	You know, thousands of soldiers fought at Truong Son. It's quite possible for there to be two people who look like each other. But please, it doesn't do any good to bring back those days. This is peace time!
NGA	Yes, that's true but, but ...
TRAN CONG	Oh Mr To. Without our yesterdays we can't have our todays, or tomorrows.
TRUNG	[*to himself*] The voice. It could be him.
TRAN CONG	[*pointing*] Mr To, is this area the market?
TO	Yes, it is.
TRAN CONG	It's too sunny! There should be roofs.
TO	Please, wear my hat.
THIET	It's okay, don't worry too much about that. Roofs feature strongly in the design of the new market.
TRAN CONG	Oh! Who's that? Who's lying there?
TO	Ah! He's a war invalid. He's mentally ill because he was wounded in the head.
TRAN CONG	What a pity! How about his parents?

Market of Lives

TO — They were both killed. His mother was killed by a B52 bomb, and his father was killed in the North Forces' offensive in 1968. Now Le is looking after him.

SONG ANH — Oh Le! I've been looking for you for so long.

LE — Song Anh.

TRAN CONG — Le, is it difficult to look after him?

LE — I love Thanh very much.

TRAN CONG — To, you have to look after these people. Oh Mr Thiet! It's so muddy, we must make the ground higher.

THIET — That's right sir! First the roof, then the ground.

NGA — Oh, we've become accustomed to the sun on our heads and our feet in the mud.

TO — Yes! As market manager I will instruct all the people to wear sandals. And wooden sandals, too! What's more I will encourage the hat sellers to sell their hats at discount prices!

TRAN CONG — Fine! But tell me, what about the layout of the market?

TO — The people who sell pig's offal and blood pudding are in that tent where you can hear the music coming from. Their products are renowned in this area sir!

TRAN CONG — Yes, they have a very good reputation.

THIET — Yes, we must give priority to national specialities. These are good, traditional products of great potential economic value.

TRAN CONG — They certainly are! And you know, this year is the year of tourism. We must have something for the foreigners to see, too.

TO — Yes sir! This is Mr Trung, who sells traditional Dong Ho pictures. He has the power of telepathy. Actually, it's more like fortune-telling. He can tell people's fortunes simply by listening to their voices, and it's always very accurate ... He also gives wonderful massages.

SONG ANH — Is it true that you have the gift of telepathy?

THIET   Fortune-telling is not acceptable! We should focus our attention on his gift of massaging.

A dog can be heard barking loudly outside.

TRAN CONG   Dogs! I'm very afraid of dogs! Don't let dogs come into the market! Too many people have died this year as a result of being bitten by rabid dogs

TRUNG   No, it isn't a dog, it sounds like Tom's voice.

Tom enters, creeping on all fours and barking like a dog.

NGA   Tom!

TOM   Mum! Here's some money!

NGA   Oh my God! Money! How did you get so much money? Tom!

TOM   Today I sold five times more newspapers than I did yesterday.

LE   Is there something sensational in the papers today?

TOM   No! Not at all. It's simple, yesterday I used words, today I tried barking, and it turns out that barking is better.

TRUNG   Why's that?

TOM   It's quite simple! Hearing me barking, people gather round to have a look. In between barking I cry out 'Newspapers' and everyone buys a paper from me. It's just like the circus or those travelling medicine shows.

TRAN CONG   Is it difficult to bark like that? Where did you learn to do that?

TOM   I'm learning it in this market, the Market of Lives! It's not hard to learn! It's very easy. Shall I show you?

NGA   I'd rather be hungry and poor and see you standing on two feet than to witness you doing such ...

TOM   If my father was at home I wouldn't be a dog. If dad wasn't a hero I wouldn't be so miserable.

Market of Lives

NGA — Tom! My son. Your father will come back soon.

TRAN CONG — Excuse me, where is your husband working? Why hasn't he returned?

NGA — Far, very far away.

SONG ANH — Dad, what can you do to help her?

TRAN CONG — Wherever he's staying, I can help you and your son to look for him.

NGA — Thankyou. But I know you can't help. He's very far away. [*Crying, and turning away.*] He only lives in my memories.

TRAN CONG — I don't understand.

TRUNG — That's his voice! That's his voice!

TO — Mr Trung! Whose voice?

TRUNG — Tran Cong's, the cadre's voice.

TRAN CONG — Why does my voice interest you so much? Do you want to tell my fortune?

TRUNG — I dare not tell yours.

SONG ANH — Please tell my father's fortune. Dad's very easy going. He was once--

TRUNG — The one who deceived his wife and children, had a son out of wedlock, and once killed someone.

TO — Oh! How dare you say such a thing. You have no evidence! On what do you base your accusation?

TRUNG — On my feelings.

TO — Mr Trung! Mr Tran Cong is a cadre of the city. You have to respect his position.

SONG ANH — Dad! Why are you so quiet? I'll cry if you don't say anything! Dad!

THANH — The truth is belonging to those who are not selfish. I would sing about my friends who live for all others.

TRAN CONG   Blind man! You'll be held responsible for what you've said.

Thanh sings in the chaotic atmosphere of the market. Lights out.

Scene Two

Tran Cong's house. Late afternoon. A large and simple room. Song Anh is engrossed in looking for something amonst some documents. Mrs Phuong, her mother, enters, silently as a shadow.

PHUONG   Oh! Song Anh! What are you looking for?

SONG ANH   Mum! Don't you know?

PHUONG   [*nervously*] What's the matter?

SONG ANH   People have been gossipping about Dad.

PHUONG   Yes. But it's just gossip. Anyone can be the subject of other peoples' talk, my dear.

SONG ANH   But this is different. There's a blind man saying that dad deceived you, mum, and has a secret son and ... has killed someone.

PHUONG   What! Where did he say that?

SONG ANH   In the market! The market dad is directing people to rebuild.

PHUONG   Deceiving me and you, and having a secret son and killing a person! Oh Anh, no, that's not true! Don't believe it! Who would dare to say such things about your father? I'll never believe it. Your father is a good man. A very good man.

SONG ANH   When Dad heard the blind man say those things, he didn't reply. And you know, he's been very strange lately. Some nights I wake up and hear him saying horrible things in his sleep, 'crows' and 'blood.' Mum, why don't you ask him what the matter is?

PHUONG   I've already asked him. He says maybe it's because in the day-time he's so busy and tired, at night he has bad dreams.

SONG ANH   Dreams often reflect what's been happening during the day. But dreams always come from inside the mind.

Market of Lives

PHUONG Don't be suspicious of him Song Anh! Life is very complicated. Now, it's quite common for someone to cook up a nasty story about someone else. Especially since your father is going to be nominated as vice chairman of the City People's Committee. You should encourage and protect your father!

SONG ANH He's a very courageous man, who once shot down a U.S. war-plane and was awarded a medal. I know that.

PHUONG He's coming back home Song Anh. Don't talk about this again.

Tran Cong enters.

TRAN CONG Good Afternoon!

SONG ANH Hi Dad!

TRAN CONG What's going on? Why does Song Anh look so edgy?

PHUONG It's that horrible story about you they've been telling in the markets.

TRAN CONG Oh, is that so? Don't pay any attention to it! It's just market-gossip. It's not important. Please, sit down here with me.

PHUONG It is important because Song Anh has got me worrying now.

TRAN CONG Oh, just sit down! There's no point in thinking about it.

PHUONG It's difficult to believe men. You spend so much time travelling, and I know it must be difficult to avoid having affairs with other women.

TRAN CONG That's not true at all!

PHUONG Then why would they invent a story like that, just to discredit you? I must hear this story first-hand.

Phuong leaves.

TRAN CONG Darling! Don't go! Don't. That fortune-teller must be arrested for the good of the city. The social and psychological implications of--

Song Anh enters and interrupts Tran Cong's speech.

SONG ANH Dad! Who are you talking to?

TRAN CONG Oh, no one, no one dear. It's just the topic of a lecture I'm giving at the Senior Citizens' conference. What's all that sugar and milk for?

SONG ANH People know you're tired, so they've brought some things for you.

TRAN CONG I've told you not to accept gifts like this. Why did you accept them? Now you have to give them all back.

SONG ANH I had no choice but to accept them. They insisted on placing them here, saying it's a sign of their affection for you.

TRAN CONG Affection? My dear, there's no such thing as affection.

The sound of Beethoven's 5th Symphony.

TRAN CONG [*nervously*] Song Anh, what horrible music that is. Turn the radio off, will you please?

SONG ANH What's the matter with you dad? That's one of Beethoven's most famous symphonies. The theme of the piece is 'Destiny'. It's been many years since we've been able to listen to Beethoven on the radio.

TRAN CONG Destiny, destiny! Turn it off! It's stuffy in here! Open all the windows, please!

Song Anh opens the windows.

SONG ANH Dad! Are you feeling any better?

TRAN CONG What's that rumbling noise?

SONG ANH Electricians. They're installing lights and banners to celebrate the elections.

TRAN CONG There's no need for so much light. Oh! Song Anh, I can hear someone crying.

SONG ANH There's a funeral at one of the houses at the end of the street. A very young soldier died. It's so sad to see all those white flowers.

TRAN CONG [*startled*] Another soldier! Dead again! Oh my dear, what's that bright red on the wall?

Market of Lives

SONG ANH	The stream of sunlight. The sun is bright, red as the eye of fire.
TRAN CONG	Oh, the eye of fire! Close the windows please!
SONG ANH	I'm afraid you'll find it stuffy again.
TRAN CONG	No, I'd rather be hot than see the eye of fire. Oh Anh, I wish we hadn't gone to the market that day.
SONG ANH	Why Dad?
TRAN CONG	So I wouldn't have heard those things.
SONG ANH	But they can't be true Dad!
TRAN CONG	No, they're not true. But it makes your mother suspect me, anyway.
SONG ANH	Dad, don't worry so much. I think Mum will believe you. I do.

Tu Du enters, carrying sausages.

TU DU	Good afternoon!
TRAN CONG	Oh, Du! Come in!
SONG ANH	Why are you carrying sausages, Tu Du?
TU DU	I know you're tired, so I've brought a gift - a couple of kilos of sausages for you.
TRAN CONG	You're too kind. Aren't writers normally a bit stingy? Don't writers never give anything away, even to their future fathers-in-law?
TU DU	Hi hi! Here's my real sign of affection! I've begun writing.
TRAN CONG	Oh, Thank you very much! You have to work hard, you know. Sausages are sausages, fathers-in-law are only fathers-in-law, but literature is for eternity.
SONG ANH	Is my job as a teacher an eternal job, Dad?
TRAN CONG	Teaching is one of the most noble professions.

TU DU	The Van Nghe newspaper is planning a special issue on the topic of war.
SONG ANH	Are you going to contribute anything?
TU DU	Yes, I am. I want to relate the experiences of my future father-in law, when he was a soldier at Truong Son in the great anti U.S. resistance. You were wounded, Mr Cong, and shot down a U.S. aeroplane. I think it will be great to write about you.
SONG ANH	Oh! You're writing about Dad. You'd better make it good.
TRAN CONG	It's a difficult thing to do. There are some things that we can never understand while we're at war. Only when it's over can we reflect on how terrible it was.
TU DU	I understand! Is it like the road-workers whose feet polished the stone on the roads, who worked at night with torches?
TRAN CONG	Maybe.
TU DU	Yes, it is the miracle which made the victory of our nation!
TRAN CONG	By the way, do you think the dead can live again?
TU DU	No, I don't think so. But why do you ask me such a strange thing?
TRAN CONG	But do you think a dead man's soul can return and inhabit another person?
TU DU	Oh! Perhaps. It depends on the advances of technology, I suppose. Are you studying the underworld?
TRAN CONG	[*coming to his senses*] Dead person! No! Er, It's the topic of a lecture I'm giving at a seminar on the development of bird-feeding in the city.
SONG ANII	Dad! Dad, what's the matter with you? What have birds got to do with dead people?
TRAN CONG	Oh! What a silly mistake! I've just remembered, that's the topic that the managing board of the Van Dien cemetery asked me to lecture on.
TU DU	You're very busy indeed.
TRAN CONG	Yes, I'm very busy. There still remain a lot of problems that we have to deal with in our society. You should write about that, about today, don't bring back

Market of Lives

	the war. It's pointless. You weren't in the war, you never fought in the war, you'll never understand it properly. Don't write about it. [*Pause*] Can I ask you something else, now? It's about murder. When you see someone else about to die, and you don't help them, is that murder?
TU DU	It depends on the situation.
TRAN CONG	Du, do you think someone with the powers of telepathy can read people's minds and know their secrets?
TU DU	I really don't know about that kind of thing
TRAN CONG	Yes! But no! Don't repeat this conversation to anyone. This time I will launch a campaign against superstition.
SONG ANH	Dad, you've been behaving so strangely lately. You've been so worried and nervous. Why are you paying so much attention to bird raising, cemeteries, Senior Citizens and campaigns against superstition? You used to do other things. You used to put a lot of effort into congratulating other people for their war efforts. Think of all the flags and certificates you gave out!
TRAN CONG	Well, of course I belong to the people. I would do anything for them.
TU DU	I will write about you as a shining example of a devoted cadre.
TRAN CONG	No! Don't write about me! Please!

Tran Cong puts his head in his hands.

SONG ANH	You must write something interesting about Dad!
TU DU	Believe me, I will immortalise our father's acts of bravery in words.

As Song Anh and Tu Du kiss, Le and Thanh enter, Thanh with a guitar, singing.

THANH	'There's a couple kissing each other by the window. Be quiet so they can kiss each other ... Birds, don't fly!'
TU DU	Oh, Le and Thanh! When did you come in?
LE	Don't get near him! He's having an epileptic fit!

THANH [*tapping Le on the cheek*] Epileptic fit? What epileptic fit? I'm just ... singing. 'Let's sing about a flame, with a very eager heart of love. Let's sing about love with a flame in your heart.'

SONG ANH Oh Le! I'm afraid when he gets like this. What should we do?

TU DU Don't worry! I'll do something about it. Hey! Good afternoon, Thanh the artist. Do you remember your old class-mate?

THANH [*singing*] 'I can never forget the soldier I met'. Attention! Artist Thanh would like to say good afternoon to Artist Tu Du. I have a new shirt, here! [*singing*] 'It is the shirt I've been wearing to remember the day...'

TU DU [*tapping Thanh on the shoulder*] That's okay, that's okay. Let's go drink some beers. We haven't been drinking with each other since we left school.

THANH 'Now we meet each other again at the inn, we're like children, even though we're twenty.'

TU DU La la la la la la la! Let's go!

Tu Du and Thanh leave, arm in arm. Le is crying.

SONG ANH Le, don't cry!

LE Today people in the market gave me some money to buy a new shirt for him. I was coming to visit you. I have some flowers for you.

SONG ANH How beautiful! Do you remember when we were still studying at school? Du and Thanh took us all the way to Ngoi Ha to buy flowers like these.

LE They're blooming now in Ngoi Ha, Song Anh.

SONG ANH Really?

LE I often take flowers to the market to sell. This is the most beautiful bouquet. I kept it specially for you.

SONG ANH How happy the days were when we were studying at school. And now... It's such a pity that Thanh is ill. Oh Le! I'd like to give you this bracelet. My father bought it overseas.

LE It's beautiful. But you should keep it, it suits your hand. It's not right for me to have it, a cleaner in the market.

Market of Lives

SONG ANH Well, I have a pair of earrings. Would you like them? I'll give them to you. They were made in France.

LE They're lovely, too. But please keep them. I can't wear them.

SONG ANH Why not?

LE When Thanh has a fit he'll snatch at them because they look strange to him.

SONG ANH Really? How's your life now?

LE Filled with tears. Thanh sings all the time, all the songs on the radio. I've made some progress with him but he's not, even for a minute, aware of what he's doing.

SONG ANH I understand. Le, why don't you find someone else?

LE So many people have asked me that. Even his father! When he was on his deathbed he started crying and he said, Le, Le, you marry someone else. Don't waste your life with Thanh. Let him be. It makes me unhappy to see you so miserable.

There is a long silence.

SONG ANH If that's what he said, why don't you respect his wishes?

LE I can't say goodbye to Thanh because I can still remember a time when we loved each other, and the songs he sang for me and his father. How he dreamed of the future, of becoming a musician. And even though his eyes look dull now, I can still see a flame in them. I believe the flame will burn more brightly.

A very long silence.

SONG ANH You can't just live in the past. You have no prospects for the future. Le! Do you understand what I'm saying? You will get older and your beauty will fade away. Le! Please understand me! You're still so beautiful.

LE Am I beautiful?

SONG ANH Yes, very beautiful. You have to think a little about yourself. You must be practical.

LE Practical! Anh, tell me what does 'practical' mean?

SONG ANH Don't you understand? It means that you can't have babies who have mental problems, who are a burden to you and to society.

LE What? Oh! Babies who ... Oh no, no!

She begins to cry. Outside, Thanh can be heard singing.

LE Oh, Thanh, he's singing again. Oh, Thanh!

Le rushes out of the house.

TRAN CONG [*offstage*] No! No! I didn't kill you! I didn't do it, it's not me. Don't laugh like that! No, forgive me, please, no, no! Go away!

SONG ANH Dad! Dad! What's the matter with you?

Anh quietly goes to look in the bedroom door. She puts her head in her hands. Blackout.

Scene Three

The market. It is raining heavily and Thanh is singing in the rain. Mrs Phuong is holding an umbrella. Thunder is rumbling in the distance.

PHUONG Where is everybody? Who can tell me why people say these things? Why my husband and no-one else? Has he really been deceiving me? Does he really have a son with someone else? Did he murder someone? No! No! He's virtuous and even-tempered man. He's never even lifted a finger against his children. Even my friends are envious of our relationship. But now what will they think? Who will offer me a word of comfort in this dark market? I can feel everyone laughing at me. Well, I'd like to ask all you wives, if you've ever loved your husband what do you do when his name is blackened? But still, there's no smoke without a fire ... Oh Cong! Is it true? No, no! Then why? Maybe they don't like you, that's why they've made up these stories Please! Rain! Wind! Keep howling! Thunder! Rumble on! Everybody listen! My husband is a good man. No-one knows this better than I do!

Phuong leaves. Later that night, the rain has stopped. It is quiet. The moon is shining brightly. Mr Trung is sitting in the middle of the market. Tom is spoon-feeding him rice soup.]

Market of Lives

TOM — Please try to eat some more to help you sweat it out. You're getting feverish again.

TRUNG — Oh, leave me alone. It's dark. Your mother will be waiting up for you. Go home!

TOM — I'm not going to leave till you finish this soup. Oh Mr Trung, why don't you come to my house? It's cold tonight, and you have a fever.

TRUNG — No, no I can't.

TOM — If you won't come with me, I'm going to sleep here with you. I can't leave you alone here at night.

TRUNG — Don't worry about me Tom. Is the moon very bright tonight?

TOM — Yes, it is.

TRUNG — The clouds are going over the moon, aren't they?

TOM — Oh yes! A black cloud looks as if it's going to swallow the moon. How did you know?

TRUNG — Because I can hear the crows crying. Long ago in Truong Son, there were nights when the moon shone brightly. But whenever the moon was covered over I heard the crows crying.

TOM — Really?

TRUNG — Yes, really! Now it's very dark! You should leave now. Tomorrow you have to sell newspapers.

TOM — Tomorrow I'll get more pictures for you to sell.

TRUNG — Yes, thanks!

TOM — Let me make your bed for you before I leave. Where's your mosquito net?

TRUNG — It's been stolen.

TOM — Damn thief! I'll bring my mosquito-net to you. Just wait a minute.

Tom runs out. A crow's cry can be heard.

TRUNG	Oh! Tom! That's the crow crying. It's a sign. I musn't make another mistake in my life.
TRAN CONG	[*walking in on tiptoe*] Mr Trung! Mr Trung!
TRUNG	[*holding his shirt pocket*] Who's that? Who's calling my name in the night?
TRAN CONG	It's me! Can you help me?
TRUNG	What? [*shouting loudly*] Don't come round pretending to be a friend and steal my money. I only have one mosquito net, and someone's already stolen it. Go away. I won't be fooled again.

Mrs Nga enters with a mosquito-net in her hands. When she sees Trang Cong she hides in the shadows.

TRAN CONG	Shhh, shhh, don't shout. It's me! I'm not here to rob you, I've just come to ask you something.
TRUNG	The voice, it's that voice again.
TRAN CONG	Yes, it's me, it's Tran Cong. You have a sharp sense of hearing and a very good memory.
TRUNG	Why did you come here at night?
TRAN CONG	I've come to see you. I'm very busy in the day-time.
TRUNG	I told you about yourself, didn't I?
TRAN CONG	Yes, you did! When I came here to survey the markets you said that I was deceiving my wife and daughter, that I had a secret child and that I murdered someone. I've been obsessed with this ever since. Now there's only me and you. Tell me, why did you say those things?
TRUNG	You were very sure of yourself back then. Now why are you trembling?

A crow cries.

TRAN CONG	Oh, I'm cold. The fog is so cold. Mr Trung, what's that sound?
TRUNG	That's a crow crying.

Market of Lives

TRAN CONG Its so frightening! Why does that sound make me tremble? Please, answer my question for my own peace of mind! Please tell me!

TRUNG Is there a scar on the left side of your chest?

TRAN CONG Yes, there is. I've had it since the war.

TRUNG Another soldier carried you on his back didn't he, through many kilometres of forest to a military hospital?

TRAN CONG Yes, that's right! But--

TRUNG Come here! Come near me! Take off your coat and kneel down.

TRAN CONG [*backing off*] Why do I have to kneel down?

TRUNG Kneel down! I want to see what your scar is like now.

TRAN CONG Here! Here's my chest.

TRUNG [*touching Tran Cong's chest*] Here it is! Here it is. I knew it, It's your voice. It's your chest. And inside your body flows the blood of an evil man. It's you, Tran Khanh.

TRAN CONG How do you know my real name?

TRUNG The scar! The scar is still here. But with a different name. Have you forgotten already? Co Tien Hill pass? Such a beautiful place!

TRAN CONG So many tears and so much blood were shed. We were surrounded by spies, U.S. planes had destroyed the strategic road.

TRUNG This road is so important! I'm the leader of our battalion.

TRAN CONG I man the machine gun. My name's Khanh Lui.

*Lui means playing truant

TRUNG I ordered you to keep the enemy down with so many volleys of gunfire.

TRAN CONG ... that I could shoot with closed eyes. I wasn't afraid of running out of bullets.

TRUNG	It was twilight. Khanh! Shoot! What are you waiting for? Shoot now or I'll kill you, I'll kill you!
TRAN CONG	Trung, hide! The Can Gao* is coming.
	Can Gao is a word referring to a particular kind of US War plane.
TRUNG	[*pushes Tran Cong out of the way and takes control of the machine gun*] Come on Can Gao, I'll blast you out of the sky!
TRAN CONG	[*hiding*] Trung, it's firing rockets at us!
TRUNG	I think I've hit it! I'll [*Trung screams and falls to the ground*] Aaaah! Khanh! It's dark! My eyes, I can't see! Help me, help! Where's the sun?
TRAN CONG	Trung, what's happened to your eyes? Did the rockets?
TRUNG	I'm blind! Khanh! Help me please!
TRAN CONG	[*pretending*] I'm, I'm wounded too!
TRUNG	Seriously? I can't carry you on my back, not this time Khanh! You can see, help me Khanh!
TRAN CONG	[*to himself*] Khanh! Think of yourself. This is your big chance! On our left is a sheer drop, on our right is the forest. Left or right, right or left? Trung! Make your way to the left ... to safety, to the left.
TRUNG	[*slides over the edge of the cliff and screams*] Aaaah! Khanh, help me! Help me, I can't feel anything with my feet. Am I going to fall? Help me, I can't hold on much longer.
TRAN CONG	Trung! You're blind! What's the point of living if you're blind?
TRUNG	Khanh, help me, have pity on me! I'm my mother's only son.
TRAN CONG	Trung! Forgive me! You're blind, you won't need anything. Better to die now.

He walks away from Trung.

TRUNG	[*screams*] You've betrayed me!

Market of Lives

He collapses.

TRAN CONG   I betrayed a friend. But from now on I won't be called Khanh Lui any more. I'll change my name to Tran Cong, and I'll take the credit for shooting down that plane. I'll be a hero.

NGA   [*from outside*] Everybody, Everybody gather round! This is Mr Khanh. A hero! He shot down a U.S. plane! He saved the military hospital, he saved the lives of hundreds of injured soldiers. Mr Khanh! I love you so much!

TRAN CONG   It wasn't me, it wasn't me!

NGA   Oh Mr Khanh, I'm so happy.

TRAN CONG   You're 'Bup May Truong Son'?*

Nga's nickname meaning the Bamboo Shoot of Truong Son.

TRUNG   So, you still remember?

TRAN CONG   No! It's not true. You're lying.

TRUNG   I didn't tell your fortune, I just told the truth.

TRAN CONG   But it wasn't me! You've got it all wrong!

TRUNG   You can change your name and your appearance, but you can't change your conscience. Wake up to yourself! You need to face the reality of what you've done.

TRAN CONG   How can a blind man in the market know this? Or has Trung's soul inhabited this old man? Then why does he look so much like Trung? Oh my God, it really is him, it's Trung. Oh Trung, forgive me! I've been praying for you all these years. I went to Truong Son to build a shrine for you by the abyss. I looked after your mother until she died. I often tell Phuong about you. Now we have a happy family and a daughter. Take pity on me! Don't hate me!

TRUNG   Phuong? A happy family? Yes, it's me Khanh, it's me, Hoang Van Trung.

TRAN CONG   But no, it can't be. How could you survive that fall? I saw your body hitting the ground.

TRUNG　　One of the mountain tribes-people rescued me and nursed me back to health.

TRAN CONG　　And now you're standing here in front of me.

TRUNG　　Yes!

TRAN CONG　　You're getting very old. And the scars have made your face look so wrinkled.

TRUNG　　I can't see what your face looks like. But I heard you panting like an animal when I unmasked you. And I can smell you. You smell like a scared man. And that's enough for me to imagine what you look like now.

TRAN CONG　　Trung! I beg you! Don't curse me! I've changed my ways. I've done so much to atone for my mistakes. I've devoted myself to serving other people. I've helped to make this nation great once more. That's why I'm here to rebuild this market.

TRUNG　　What will you name the market?

TRAN CONG　　What? Hasn't it already got a name?

TRUNG　　Ah, yes! Cho Doi, Market of Lives - that's its name. But you must remember that its foundations should be honesty, purity and kindness, not lies and deception.

TRAN CONG　　I know, I know. People believe in me. People are relying on me to rebuild this market.

TRUNG　　You don't deserve their trust. You know you should confess to your crimes, otherwise you're deceiving them.

The cry of a crow can be heard.

TRAN CONG　　It's that crow's cry again. How can I make it stop?

TRUNG　　Only the arrival of the daylight will stop the crow calling.

TRAN CONG　　No, don't force me to confess. My reputation will be destroyed. Everything I've done will come to nothing.

TRUNG　　You haven't changed. You once tried to kill your friend to advance your position. Now you're betraying people's trust in you by building a market to get

Market of Lives

TRAN CONG: their support, so once again you can improve your standing in the community. You're always thinking of yourself, never of others.

TRAN CONG: Let me be your servant. I'll do anything you want. I'll give you a job, a house ... How about a trip overseas?

TRUNG: Such a bad man, his mind never changes.

TRAN CONG: Please, please don't force me to confess.

TRUNG: It's too easy to keep on deceiving people if you don't confess now.

TRAN CONG: Oh Trung! Why? Why are you threatening me? Why do you want me to change everything for you? What for? Why?

TRUNG: For everyone else's sake. For the future of this market, you have to confess.

TRAN CONG: [*picking up a stone*] I will--

TRUNG: You can never kill me again. Years ago, you wanted to kill me in the forest. Now you want to kill me in the markets.

TRAN CONG: I will make my confession in front of everyone, I swear. But you, you must never tell them who you are. Just keep on being the blind man who sells pictures in the market, forever.

TRUNG: Why? Why should I do that?

TRAN CONG: Because I don't want Phuong to hate me. We've been happily married for years. Don't dig up my terrible past in front of her! It will only upset her. You belong in the past as far as she's concerned.

TRUNG: Phuong! Yes! Yes! Never! Yes! Leave me!

Tran Cong goes as Mrs Nga rushes in.

NGA: Trung! I was bringing a mosquito-net for you and I heard what was going on! It's me! I was Bup May Truong Son! How come we didn't we recognise each other? Why didn't you recognise me?

TRUNG: Nga! Is that Nga?

NGA   Why didn't we recognise each other?

TRUNG   Pain has changed us. But why are you living here, in this place?

NGA   I've been looking for someone, just like you. And imagine, it's the same man we're looking for!

TRUNG   Is he Tran Cong?

NGA   Yes! I recognised him when he came to the market that first time. I was going to rush up to him and hug him. I was going to say, 'Tom, this is your father. Come and see your father.'

TRUNG   Why didn't you? It would've made Tom happy? Is Tom really his son?

NGA   Yes, just after the fighting I concealed the truth because he was about to be awarded a medal for being a hero. And a hero can never make a mistake, even if it's only a mistake caused by love.

TRUNG   Is that so?

NGA   Even when I met him in the market I couldn't stop thinking 'He's a hero'. And no hero should have a son pretending to be a dog so he can sell his newspapers, and a poor wife who has to sell herbal medicine in the market.

TRUNG   Nga! In my mind, you're just like you used to be in Truong Son.

NGA   No this time I won't hide the truth I'll confront him. I'll let everyone know who he is and what he's done.

TRUNG   No, Nga, don't do that! For Phuong's sake! Don't tell the truth! You'll spoil everything for her. She has a happy family, as good a life as any woman could hope for. She believes in her husband. She'll be so unhappy if she knows the truth. Let her think she's happy. Nga please don't denounce him.

NGA   Trung! Alright I won't do it. I won't denounce him. For you.

Nga and Trung stand under the bright moonlight. Blackout.

Scene Four

Morning in Tran Cong's house. Phuong is worried. She is waiting for someone to phone. Tu Du is sitting by the table, writing.

TU DU 'The soldiers set forth to Truong Son to liberate the country and drive out the enemy.' Yes! That sounds great!

PHUONG Du! Have some lunch! You've been writing since this morning, you must be hungry.

TU DU Yes, but don't worry about it. I've got something interesting here. Oh! The image I have of your husband at Truong Son is very clear in my mind. Let me read this passage for you!

PHUONG Yes, read it please!

TU DU 'There's one man from Ha Noi, destined to be a hero, marching with the troops along Truong Son'.

PHUONG Oh yes, that's it.

TU DU 'His first name is Cong and his family name is Tran. He's thinking of the girl he loves. A girl with long hair and eyes as blue as the water in Truc Bach Lake.'

PHUONG That's a good start. But shouldn't reveal his name first off. And secondly, the eyes should be described as 'blue as the water in Autumn.' It's more poetic.

TU DU Ah yes, good point, I'll correct that.

PHUONG Please, continue!

TU DU 'In extremely difficult conditions, oblivious to pain and hardship, our soldier lays waste to the enemy's planes.'

PHUONG Don't you think it's a little strong?

TU DU Oh, leave it like that. The editorial board will tone it down.

PHUONG Have you written about what was happening back at home?

TU DU		Yes, I've written a section called, 'Letter from the Front-Line Covered With Tears.'
PHUONG		And you know, at that you point you should be talking about the war planes.
TU DU		[*writing it down*] Yes, yes. 'One after another the bombers . . .
PHUONG		But what was it like on the ground when the planes were coming? I wasn't there.
TU DU		Neither was I. Ah! I remember, I read somewhere that someone described it as a rain of bombs, falling.
PHUONG		Well yes, of course there were a lot of bombs falling, but you need a strong image to convey what it was like on the ground.
TU DU		Ah yes. Ah, what about Sapindus fruits falling? Oh I like that, 'Bombs falling like Sapindus fruits.'
PHUONG		And the soldier was wounded on his left chest.
TU DU		[*taking notes*] His left breast.
PHUONG		He still bears the scar.
TU DU		On your husband's left breast.
PHUONG		Why are you writing that?
TU DU		Oh!
PHUONG		And now what are you going to write?
TU DU		It's only the first draft. Part one of the memoirs. The next scene is fire-crackers, flowers, decorative lighting, cheering, adulation. The elections. I've got it all in my mind. 'His greatest triumph'. It'll be a fantastic scene.
PHUONG		As it should be. The elections are close at hand. These memoirs will put a stop to those nasty rumours.
TU DU		Don't worry. As soon as Mr Cong agrees to it, we can publish the memoirs. Oh! I've got to go. There's a professor giving a lecture today on Honesty in Literature.

Market of Lives

PHUONG Oh! Hurry up, off you go, otherwise you'll be late.

TU DU Bye!

Tu Du goes quickly. Trung appears at the door.

PHUONG Who are you?

TRUNG Excuse me, is this Tran Cong's house?

PHUONG Yes, it is. Do you want to see him?

TRUNG I'm the blind man from the market, I sell pictures. Were you looking for me a few days ago?

PHUONG Oh! Are you that man?

TRUNG Yes, I am.

PHUONG Please, sit down, here's a chair.

TRUNG Thank you. What did you want to see me for?

PHUONG [*getting all fired up*] Why have you been spreading such malicious rumours about my husband?

TRUNG Malicious rumours?

PHUONG Yes. My husband is a cadre, much respected in the community. Why did you try to humiliate him like that?

TRUNG Humiliate?

PHUONG Yes. Don't you understand? My husband's good reputation is being questioned because of your stories. You think the sound of someone's voice can tell you everything about them. Well it can't. The voice can't tell you anything.

TRUNG The voice can help people to recognise each other.

PHUONG When I listen to your voice, I hear the voice of someone who wants to make people unhappy.

TRUNG   I don't mean to hurt you. Your voice I think you must sing beautifully. But only sad songs.

PHUONG   Are you telling my fortune? Well, it's true, when I was young, I used to love singing sad songs. 'Giot Mua Thu' - Rain in Autumn.

TRUNG   Is the line, 'a life is a sea of troubles', in that song?

PHUONG   Yes, it is. Go on! Why are you so quiet?

TRUNG   Is it raining outside? I can hear the sound of raindrops falling into a small glass fish-pond, with rock work in the middle.

PHUONG   [*going to the window*] You have wonderful hearing. It really is raining. And the glass basin is there, but the rock work is broken. But how did you know there was a glass fish-pond in the garden of my house?

TRUNG   I had an image of it in my mind It just turns out to be true.

PHUONG   It's true. But long ago when I was young ... Oh! I nearly forgot, would you like some water? Some coffee? I'll pour some coffee for you.

TRUNG   Just hearing you speak now, I can tell you're thinking about something in the past.

PHUONG   Yes, but they're just memories. From long, long ago. Please, drink the coffee.

TRUNG   You make very nice coffee. Perhaps you used to make coffee for your parents? Very thick, with no sugar.

PHUONG   [*surprised*] Listening to you I feel like what you've said about my husband might be true ... I wonder if it could ...

TRUNG   No, you shouldn't think about it.

PHUONG   If it's true, you'll have to tell me why you said those things.

TRUNG   Do you really need to know?

PHUONG   Yes, I do. Because I believe my husband is a good man.

Market of Lives

TRUNG — Well you should believe him. A wife needs to be able to trust her husband.

PHUONG — Then why did you humiliate him? You can tell the truth about rain and coffee, but what you said about my husband is much more important. I don't believe it. Do you hate him?

TRUNG — No, don't think like that, please!

PHUONG — But why?

TRUNG — I ... I may have mistaken him for someone else.

PHUONG — Oh! Why are you crying! I'm sorry.

TRUNG — It's just, it's just I have an image of you in my mind, crying. Your shining eyes, your long dark hair, your delicate cheekbones. Long ago! Long ago there was a man who wanted to paint your beauty, like Michelangelo painting Venus. And then the war! Everything changed. And you pushed those memories down, memories of a youth who once loved you, but had to go and fight for his country ... and never returned to marry you.

PHUONG — Oh my God! That's exactly. How did you know? You seem to have an understanding... How could you know these things about my past? Who are you?

TRUNG — I'm a fortune teller.

PHUONG — But what you've said brings back so many painful memories. It's true, the war took my love from me, and broke my heart.

TRUNG — He wasn't killed by bombs or bullets. He was betrayed.

PHUONG — I didn't betray him. He wanted to paint me but then the war came, and he went to the front ... I thought I'd never lose him. I kept leaves in books to count the days he was away. I waited for him! I waited and waited, until Tran Cong appeared in the last days of the war. He had a medal for bravery pinned to his chest, and he told me my lover had been killed.

TRUNG — And you believed him?

PHUONG — Yes. I was so unhappy, and he made me believe he could replace my lover. I needed to believe in something. And he was a hero, devoted to his country.

TRUNG   So different.

PHUONG   Why do you say that? Do you know them?

TRUNG   No, I don't.

PHUONG   Looking at you, your mouth, your nose I feel like you're him. You're so like him!

TRUNG   No, no! You're mistaken. I'm just a blind man who sells pictures in the market.

PHUONG   It is you! How could I not recognise you? Trung! That explains everything. You're Trung!

Tran Cong enters.

TRAN CONG Oh! What are you doing here? What have you been telling my wife?

TRUNG   I told her that I was wrong. I mistook you for someone else.

TRAN CONG Are you sure it's a mistake?

TRUNG   Yes.

TRAN CONG Phuong, what did he tell you? You know my life is devoted to you.

PHUONG   Cong! I'm confused, Cong! Don't you think he looks a lot like Trung?

TRAN CONG Trung? Who's Trung? Ah, Yes Maybe. Maybe a little bit like him. Trung's nose was higher, Trung's eyes were nicer. Don't talk of the dead, let him rest in peace.

PHUONG   No! Look at him carefully! It's him. I don't believe he died. I don't.

Phuong runs out.

TRAN CONG What did you tell her?

TRUNG   The past! The past made sad and bitter by your deception.

TRAN CONG The past, the past! Did she recognise you?

Market of Lives

TRUNG I don't know. How could I know?

TRAN CONG I thought we had an agreement. Keep quiet. Do you want to destroy my family?

TRUNG You're afraid of the truth!

TRAN CONG That's not the point. I want everything to be okay until after the election.

TRUNG The people will be fooled again. It means that.

TRAN CONG You don't understand anything. You can't do certain things if you're a politician. Leave my life alone. Don't ruin my career.

TRUNG I'll keep my word. But you must do this - just before voting begins you must make your confession in front of the people. You can't mislead the children of the market. Future generations must know the truth. I want you to come clean. So does your conscience, Tran Cong.

TRAN CONG Never! Hoang Van Trung, I will never confess! You can go and denounce me. But watch out, you might be accused of slander.

TRUNG I believe in justice.

TRAN CONG Of course, everyone believes in justice. But what evidence do you have that I'm guilty? Do you have any at all? Only you and I what happened in the Truong Son jungle. No one will believe you. So be careful, Trung. No-one will even believe you're still alive.

TRUNG What? What? Is there nobody here to believe me? Why is it so quiet?

TRAN CONG [*smiling*] See? Nobody.

TRUNG She is. Only her.

TRAN CONG Who?

TRUNG Her.

TRAN CONG I'll make sure she never knows you're still alive. Go away Trung.

Trung leaves. The sound of a stick on the street can be heard outside.

TRAN CONG	Trung, wait, don't go. I was angry. I'm sorry.

Mr To rushes in.

TO	Oh, here you are Mr Cong. It's so tense down in markets. I can't stand it any longer. I've come to resign as market manager.
TRAN CONG	What's going on?

Song Anh returns from school.

SONG ANH	Good-morning Mr To. Hi Dad! What's happened!
TO	My God, the market is in chaos. Understand?

Thanh's voice can be heard from outside gradually receding.

THANH	Mr Cong, the market is dispersing, the market is dispersing, Mr Cong!
TO	Oh, that weirdo! Shut up, take a hike!
SONG ANH	[*calls out*] Thanh!
TRAN CONG	Mr To, what do you mean, 'chaos'?
TO	The gamblers were fighting over some money, and a huge brawl developed.
TRAN CONG	Is everybody alright?
TO	One dead, two injured. They're still slugging it out down there, I think.
TRAN CONG	Keep calm. Sit down.
TO	How can I be calm in this situation? Yesterday, a young girl deliberately walked three times around the market without her trousers, for a few thousand dong. The handcart men bet her to do it. When I got there, she kept walking another round before she put her trousers back on.
SONG ANH	That explains what happened when I was doing teacher training at the primary school yesterday. When I began talking about the two National heroines, Vo Thi Sau and Ut Tich, the pupils started laughing uncontrollably. It's so important to instil in them proper moral values.

TRAN CONG	Don't blame the children. It's your duty to teach them what's wrong and what's right. But when they grow up, they have to make their own choices.
SONG ANH	Well, is that so?
TO	That's not all. An iron-smuggler, in love with the girl who sells noodles, stole his mother's gold to give to the girl just the other day. The mother found out and there was a huge fight right in the middle of the market.
SONG ANH	Really?
TO	And there's more. An old beggar threw a handful of mud into another man's bowl of noodle soup, just because the man didn't give him any money. And then the man forced the poor old beggar to eat it.
TRAN CONG	The new market is finished, but the old one is shambles. How come all these things have happened? You're supposed to be in charge.
TO	Well I'm a very busy man. I can't take care of everything. I can't read people's minds. How can I tell if this man or that man is going to do something stupid?
TRAN CONG	Where is your revolutionary will?
TO	For God's sake, don't mention revolutionary will at a time like this. You know, my best friend lives near Hang Co Station, but I daren't go to see him because I'm so afraid of the thieves and gangsters in that area. All I can do is write him letters. [*Tran Cong and Mr To both laugh.*]
TRAN CONG	Well, you may as well go now.

Tom rushes in.

TOM	Mr To! Mr To! Trung is dead!
TO	What?
TOM	The gamblers were fighting, and one of them waved a huge knife around.
TO	And then what happened?
TOM	Mr Trung threw himself into the fight, trying to stop them. And he's blind, so he couldn't see anything.

TO   Oh my God!

TOM   I got there too late. He was bleeding everywhere.

TO   Oh, Mr Trung!

SONG ANH   Dad, I'm so frightened!

TRAN CONG   Mr To, you'll prepare a suitable burial for the poor man, won't you?

TO   Yes, I will.

All except Tran Cong leave.

TRAN CONG   Trung! That's the end. All my troubles will leave with you now. But why did you behave like you did? You're so stupid. How could you tell people what to do? Who are you to advise people in this mad life?

Tran Cong laughs a satisfied but bitter laugh. The voice of Thanh can be heard outside.

THANH   Ha ha ha, be so foolish. All your friends are still there, you know? Your lover's there, too. Then you'll have to leave them all. Oh, time goes by. A man's footprints will fade.

Scene Five

The market at night. Everything is lying about in disarray. In the centre is a shrine for Trung. It is cold and quiet. Tran Cong sits at the shrine. Phuong quietly enters and hides behind the shrine.

TRAN CONG   Trung! Why did this happen to you? Why couldn't you live to tell everybody that what you said about me was wrong. The elections are tomorrow. How will people trust me, now? Why aren't you still alive? If you were still alive I could make up for what I've done. You came and went, and now people think I'm a criminal. Trung! I'm not guilty. We used to be best friends in the old days. All this is because of the war. Just one cowardly mistake has ruined my life ... Trung! You've led a noble life and died out of love for your fellow human beings. I beg your soul to help the new market. The new market will put the past to rest, both the war and our story. Trung, please witness my honesty.

A group of people circles around Tran Cong, representing his conscience.

TRAN CONG   Who are you? Past, present or future?

Market of Lives

NGA   You can never bury the past. It always leaves its trace on the present. You can't wipe it away. Trung has died, but we are still living, and other will live after us. To die and live mean nothing. Maybe when a man dies he can leave everything, forget about everything, but he can't run away from himself while he's alive.

TRUNG   Life is life. And remember that this life must be built on the foundations of purity, goodwill and a clean conscience, not deception, dishonesty and selfish pride.

TOM   Mum, I've earned money from this damn newspaper to help you. Why are you angry at me?

NGA   Tom, my dear, you can't see this life clearly if you live it like a dog.

LE   There is no reason to keep him believing that this muddy drain is a beautiful garden and that this street market is paradise.

SONG ANH   Dad, I'll have to tell my pupils the truth, so that they'll see they must build a better society.

The circle of people disappears. The dream ends.

TRAN CONG   Where are you? Where? Trung? Is that your people who are speaking?

Dawn. A boy somewhere is crying out 'newspapers'. Tom enters.

TOM   Papers, papers! Here's the latest news! Market to be rebuilt! Election of the people's committee today. Good morning, Mr Cong. Do you want a newspaper? Why are you here so early? Look, your hair's all wet with mist.

TRAN CONG   Give me a newspaper, boy.

TOM   Here you are. Oh, why did you put it there?

TRAN CONG   So that Mr Trung can read it too.

Mr To enters with Mrs Nga.

TO   As the market manager, I order you to take away this shrine.

NGA   I won't let you!

TO	Why not? We all feel sorry about what happened to Mr Trung, but this shrine is taking up valuable space. Get rid of it.
TRAN CONG	What's the problem, Mr To?
TO	Oh, you're here. You can help me deal with this. This situation is intolerable.

Thiet rushes in.

THIET	Cong, where were you last night? Everybody's looking for you.

Song Anh and Tu Du walk in.

SONG ANH	Dad, where have you been?
TU DU	Good morning Mr Cong.
TRAN CONG	Good morning. I was here.
TU DU	This will be a precious detail for the memoirs.
TO	Oh, Mr Cong, They're coming. It's going to be so crowded.
TRAN CONG	Who?
TO	Well, this shrine was set up by Mrs Nga. It occupies the space assigned to Mrs Nga, but also Mrs Thin, who sells boiled shell-fish. Mrs Thin wants to get rid of it, while Mrs Nga doesn't. And as a result, the whole market is taking sides. Early this morning, Mrs Thin went to her village to fetch some men. Here they come!
TU DU	Take it down, Mr Cong. He wasn't a hero.
THIET	Cong? I'd like to say how unsightly it is. When the new market is finished, how can you keep this here?

Some big men enter.

TO	Look here they come! Do something, Mr Cong!
NGA	I beg you. Please show him some respect. Don't do that. He was blind because of you all and died because of you all. Why do you begrudge him this tiny piece of land?

Market of Lives

TOM — No-one can touch it.

TO — Mr Cong.

TRAN CONG — To, bring me some joss-sticks.

TO — Yes.

TRAN CONG — Be quick.

TO — Here you are.

TRAN CONG — My friends, we'll erect a memorial here on which we'll write very clearly, 'This is the worship place of Mr Hoang Van Trung, the hero of Truong Son'.

NGA — Trung, I'm still afraid that you won't keep your promise.

TRAN CONG — Who are you?

NGA — It's me, Bup May Truong Son.

TRAN CONG — What? You?

NGA — Yes, it's me. I recognised you the first day you came to the market. But you didn't recognise me. Cong, this is Tom. He's your son. You can't ignore him now. He's part of the future of this market, and he's our child. He was born when we were both young, during the war.

TRAN CONG — Tom?

NGA — That night in Truong Son jungle. Don't you remember? Tom, come here. This is your father.

TRAN CONG — Oh God, another one. My past is haunting me today.

NGA — No, it's your conscience haunting you. Be brave. Just for once in your life. Tom, come to your father.

SONG ANH — Dad, is this true? Everything the poor blind man said was true?

TRAN CONG — Yes my dear. It's the truth.

SONG ANH	What am I going to tell my pupils tomorrow? What am I going to make them believe in now?
TRAN CONG	Please forgive me my dear.
SONG ANH	Dad, how can I believe in you now?
TU DU	The memoirs, I've spent so much time over them. I'm up to page 327!
TRAN CONG	Burn them, Du. It's all lies.

Everyone jumps when suddenly Phuong appears from behind the shrine.

PHUONG	Trung. Why didn't you recognise me? Why? I've been waiting for you for so long. [*To Tran Cong*] I've followed you and hidden behind this shrine to hear you confessing everything. [*To Trung*] Why didn't you recognise me? [*To Tran Cong*] You've made my life so miserable and bitter. *Pause.*
TRAN CONG	Phuong. Please, call down curses upon me, but don't look at me like that.

Tran Cong leaves, dejectedly.

THIET	[*following Tran Cong*] Cong!
SONG ANH	Dad, wait for me!
PHUONG	He's gone. Look, he's disappearing in a cloud of dust. I believed in him my whole life. I thought I was important to him. I just existed to be a part of his life. I was wrong.
TU DU	We are living in strange and stormy times. Everybody, let's get together and build the new market! I'll write about this market, and this time I'll write the truth about it.

The market becomes boisterous. To is whistling, then he stops.

TO	Be quiet, be quiet. Do you hear anything? It's funny old Thanh singing. Well, how beautifully he sings today! There, can you hear him?
THANH	'My country in streamlined shape/Hearing the tender voice of our motherland/ In her struggles against the invaders/The people who will never come home/ Their mothers cry quietly.' **THE END**

Journey to the West

LEE CHEE KENG

Lee Chee Keng was born in Singapore in 1972. He is a member of Practice Theatre's Chinese Play-Writing Studio, as well as TheatreWorks' English Writers' Lab. He has had several plays produced in Singapore and has published a volume of his Chinese prose and poetry. He is presently a student at the National University of Singapore.

My special thanks to Ho Kah Wai, Kala Anandarajah, Sharon Lim, Noraizah Nordin and Enrico Varella. Also to Krishen Jit and Lok Meng Chue, Robin Loon, and everyone in TheatreWorks.

CHARACTERS

> BEN/SUN WU KONG
> A/SHA ZHEN
> B/MASTER/BEN'S MOTHER/BEN'S FATHER
> C/ADVISER/GIRL/OLD MAN
> D/KING/BA JIE
>
> A,C,D, together as BUDDHA

SETTING

Two-faced puppets were used throughout the first production of the play. One face of the puppet would be used when the actors are playing themselves, and the other when they are playing the Chinese legend 'Journey To The West'. Lighting design also helps to establish the different dimensions in the play. There is no props use, and the 'realities' of the play is expressed through body movements of the actors.

Structurally, the play make extensive use of the analogy between 'Journey To The West', a popular Chinese legend, and the 'life stories' of Ben. In this text, the word 'SHIFT' indicates a pause or mood change.

Ben is being locked up in his house. The other children are playing outside his house, acting out scenes from 'Journey To The West'.

	A	O, ugly monster, you have nowhere to escape.
	BEN	There is so much space under the heavens, why are you after my blood?
	C	I can't leave you to harm the human race.
	D	I'll have to deal with you today.
	BEN	[*in Mandarin*] I will run away.

SHIFT. *The children become aware that Ben is actually being locked up.*

	C	Master, there is something trapped under the mountain.
	D	What is it?

Journey to the West

	C	It looks like a monster, but I think it is a monkey.
	D	A monkey trapped under a mountain?
	A	Master, master.
	C	It can speak our language, it must be a very clever monkey.
	D	Who are you?
	BEN	[*in Mandarin*] I am the monkey king. I created havoc in heaven, fought with all the gods, and was trapped under this mountain. I was told that a monk going to the West will pass this way, I'm suppose to escort him to the West.
B [*as master*]		Good. Then you shall come out, together we'll go to the west.
	BEN	[*in Mandarin*] You have to retreat a little, so that I will not hurt you when I come out of this mountain.
B [*as master*]		Come out, and I shall call you Sun Wu Kong.
SHIFT.	Ben	I can't come out.
	C	Why can't you fly out from under the mountain?
	BEN	I can't, I have been locked in the house.
	B	You have never played with us.
	BEN	I want to play with you.
	D	Every time we ask you to come out, you say you can't.
	BEN	I can't come out. It's not that I don't want to.
	B	Just say if you don't want to play with us.
	BEN	I want to come out and play with you. My mother won't let me out.
	A	Why is your mother like that?

D	Don't want to play with you any more.
BEN	I want to come out and play.
B	No fun playing with you.
C	Cannot fly how you be Sun Wu Kong?
BEN	If you're so clever, then you be Sun Wu Kong.
C	But you always play Sun Wu Kong.
BEN	But I cannot come out.
A	OK, we'll try to help you out.
C	How?
D	We can use my super soaker.

The children try to shoot open the door with their Super Soaker water gun.

BEN	It's not working, and you wet my floor.
B	What can we do now?
D	I don't know.
BEN	Quick, think.
A	I know, we can use the magic key on my crown.
BEN	OK, quick.

They try the magic key. Light change. Ben is out of the house.

C	He is out. Master, what shall we do now?
B [*as master*]	Together we'll go to the West.

In an operatic manner, they embark on their journey to the West. All except Ben freeze. This happens whenever Ben narrates scenes from 'Journey to the West'.

Journey to the West

BEN   Sun Wu Kong and the others journey to the West, and reach a country where they meet the king.

SHIFT.

BEN [*as Sun Wu Kong*]   [*in Mandarin*] How can you say that we are demons?

B [*as master*]   Do not be rude.

D [*as king*]   My state advisers are always right. They said you should be captured.

BEN [*as Sun Wu Kong*]   [*in Mandarin*] How do you know they are not demons themselves?

D [*as king*]   They look like normal human beings, but you're not.

B [*as master*]   My disciples have many powers, but they have good heart.

D [*as king*]   Good, there will be a rain making competition between you and my state advisers. If you win, you will go free, if you lose, you're dead men.

The state adviser steps out. He acknowledges the four directions as he gives his instructions.

C [*as adviser*]   I will cry four times. At the first cry, wind will come; at the second, clouds will come; at the third, thunder will sound; at the forth, rain will fall. I will cry once more and the rain will stop.

The state adviser cries. The thunder storm is portrayed by the body movements of the actors.

BEN [*as Sun Wu Kong*]   [*in Mandarin*] Who is in charge of these elements? Bring them back.

The thunder storm stops.

BEN [*as Sun Wu Kong*]   [*in Mandarin*] Why are you helping them? Listen, here are my orders. When I point my cudgel upwards once, a blast of wind. Twice, clouds and mist. The third time, thunder and lightning. The forth, rain. And at the fifth time, the storm must cease.

D [*as king*]   Enough, no more rain, or the crops will be ruined.

SHIFT.

BEN Sun Wu Kong was more powerful. The king freed them and they move on. But before they set off, the master lectures Sun Wu Kong.

SHIFT.

B [*as master*] You must always know when to stop. If I had not stopped you, many innocent people would have been killed. A priest must never kill.

SHIFT.

B [*as Ben's mom*] Why are you back so late?

BEN I went to the kindergarten with Hui Ling to pick Up her younger brother.

B [*as mom*] I said you have to be home by six.

BEN I know.

B [*as mom*] What time is it now?

BEN Six-thirty.

B [*as mom*] You never do as I say.

BEN Nobody is home before four, and you won't give me the house keys.

B [*as mom*] You don't want to come home any more?

BEN No.

Mom Then you'd better behave yourself.

BEN You are always telling me what to do.

B [*as mom*] I know what is good. I have come a long way. You have to learn.

SHIFT.

BEN The journey to the west continues, and they walk into a mountainous area.

SHIFT.

B [*as master*] Wu Kong, I'm hungry. Can you go and see if you can get some food?

Journey to the West

BEN [*as Sun Wu Kong*]	I'll fly to the village. [*To the other disciples*] You take good care of the master.
SHIFT.	
BEN	After Sun Wu Kong left, a very pretty girl approaches.
SHIFT.	
D [*as Ba Jie*]	Wow, there's someone coming.
C [*as girl*]	Where are you heading?
B [*as master*]	We're heading for the West. Why are you traveling alone?
C [*as girl*]	I'm sending lunch to my husband. He works on a farm on the other side of the mountain.
D [*as Ba Jie*]	We have food now.
A [*as Sha Zhen*]	Wu Kong is taking so long.
B [*as master*]	Do not be rude. [*To girl*] Isn't it dangerous for you to walk alone?
SHIFT.	
BEN	Sun Wu Kong returns. He could tell straight away that she is actually the white skeleton demon He kills her right off.

SHIFT. A little struggle from the girl, but Sun Wu Kong kills her without much difficulty.

D [*as Ba Jie*]	Master, Wu Kong has killed the girl.
B [*as master*]	How can you do that?
BEN [*as Sun Wu Kong*]	[*in Mandarin*] She's a monster. She would have eaten you up.
D [*as Ba Jie*]	How can such a pretty girl be a monster?
A [*as Sha Zhen*]	You're just as evil as before.

The master chants, and Sun Wu Kong gets a deadly headache.

BEN [*as Sun Wu Kong*]	[*in Mandarin*] Please, master, do not chant anymore. I can't take this any more.

B [*as master*]	The golden band you wear on your head will tighten every time I chant. This is the only way I can punish you.
BEN [*as Sun Wu Kong*]	[*in Mandarin*] I did not do anything wrong.
B [*as master*]	You have just done the worst of all evil deeds. You never want to learn.
BEN [*as Sun Wu Kong*]	[*in Mandarin*] Look at the food she's bringing for her husband, all snakes and frogs.
D [*as Ba Jle*]	He must have used his magic to change the food into these horrible creatures.
BEN [*as Sun Wu Kong*]	[*in Mandarin*] Master, you must believe me.
B [*as master*]	You'd better behave yourself. You're always so troublesome.
BEN [*as Sun Wu Kong*]	[*in Mandarin*] I know what I'm doing.
SHIFT. **BEN**	They continue their journey. The monster did not die. She came back in another form.

The 'girl' lying dead on the ground transforms into another demon.

D [*as Ba Jle*]	Look, there's an old lady coming this way.
A [*as Sha Zhen*]	Must be the mother of the girl Wu Kong has just killed.
BEN	Sun Wu Kong does not waste time. He kills the old woman.

SHIFT. *The old woman struggles a little, but Sun Wu Kong kills her easily.*

B [*as master*]	How can you come with me if you keep killing all the people we meet?

[*He starts chanting*]

BEN [*as Sun Wu Kong*]	[*in Mandarin. He is in pain.*] But master, she is a monster.

Journey to the West

B [*as master*] You must never kill. I have come a long way from China. You have to learn if you want to attain wisdom.

SHIFT.

BEN The master chants every time. That's all he knows. Only Sun Wu Kong can tell who is really a monster. Maybe it's because he had created havoc and fought with all the gods. They worship these gods. They can never see.

SHIFT.

D [*as Ba Jie*] Look, an old man is coming this way.

A [*as Sha Zhen*] Wu Kong has killed his wife and daughter, we're in deep trouble.

B [*as master*] Why are you travelling alone?

C [*as old man*] I'm looking for my wife. I asked her to go out and look for our daughter.

BEN [*as Sun Wu Kong*] Why can't you do it yourself?

C [*as old man*] I don't usually do such things.

BEN You just don't care.

C [*as old man*] I am busy, I have to work.

BEN You only care about money, simply can't be bothered with your children.

C [*as old man*] I'm training them to be independent. I can't be there all the time.

BEN You have never shown that you care.

C [*as old man*] They should know that I do care. I brought them up.

BEN You ugly monster.

Wu Kong kills the old man.

B [*as master*] How can you kill everyone we meet?

He starts chanting.

BEN	[*in Mandarin*] I cannot let these devils stay.
B [*as master*]	Everything exists for a good purpose.
BEN	[*in Mandarin*] They will eat you up.
B [*as master*]	You can never change. Go, go back to your caves.
BEN	[*in Mandarin*] Why can't you believe me?
B [*as master*]	Get back to your caves.

SHIFT. Ben sits in one corner.

B [*as Ben's dad*]	Why are you sitting there alone?
BEN	I'm just alone.
B [*as dad*]	Don't see you studying at all.
BEN	You're not home most of the time, how do you see me study?
B [*as dad*]	You always go out until very late, where do you find time to study? Are you playing with puppets again?
BEN	Yes.
B [*as dad*]	Will puppets earn you any money?
BEN	All you care about is money. Ya, puppets won't earn me any money, and I'll die of hunger.
B [*as dad*]	I work very hard at the Chinese medicine hall. If I have no money, how can I feed you? Where do you get your clothes, get to go to school? [*Pause.*] There you go, keeping quiet again. Can't even talk to me for a short while. I won't bother you any more.
BEN	I've never asked you to be bothered.
B [*as dad*]	Ah Wai, remember who you're talking to, I'm your father. Is that what you've learned from your puppets?
BEN	What has it got to do with my puppets?

Journey to the West

B [*as dad*]   All you artist types are the same.

BEN   What the same?

B [*as dad*]   All low class people, people who can't do well in any other thing. Just act and hope that people will give you money.

BEN   That is what people thought in the past. It's not like that now.

B [*as dad*]   What's the difference? It's in the papers today, you artists are begging the government for more money, so that you can sit around and make merry. All you do is complain that the government is not giving you enough money.

BEN   You don't understand.

B [*as dad*]   Yes, I don't understand why you have to join the artists. If you have time, why don't you come to the medicine hall and help me?

BEN   Why can't you let me do what I want?

B [*as dad*]   I don't want you to go out begging.

BEN   I won't.

B [*as dad*]   You will have to run the medicine hall one day.

BEN   Why can't you let me do what I want?

B [*as dad*]   What will people say when they see you begging in public?

BEN   I can do anything I want with the puppets.

B [*as dad*]   All those ugly puppets of yours, see if I don't throw away your puppets one day.

BEN   They are mine.

B [*as dad*]   Why are you staring at me like that? Those ugly puppets, I have never seen such things before.

BEN   I made them myself. Go in and see if there is anything in the room that is being bought with your money.

B [*as dad*]	I can throw away anything in my house.
BEN	Try, just try and see what will happen. The story of 'Journey To The West' has it that Sun Wu Kong and the rest finally reached the west and got the scriptures. Actually, I'd rather the story ends with Sun Wu Kong going back to his caves. He can do anything he wants, why go to the West?

SHIFT.

BEN [*as Sun Wu Kong*]	[*in Mandarin*] Master, we have reached the Holy Mountain. We have to cross the River of Clouds.
B [*as master*]	That is my body floating down the river. Am I dead?
BEN [*as Sun Wu Kong*]	[*in Mandarin*] You are rid of your earthly body. You'll have wisdom on the further shores. Look at this realm of flowers and cranes. Isn't it better than your haunted deserts where there were only hardships and terrors?
B [*as master*]	That is Buddha on the Holy Mountain.

Sun Wu Kong and the master bow to the Buddha.

A, C, D [*as Buddha*]	Holy priest, you have shown true devotion, and shall be 'Buddha Of Precious Merit'. Sun Wu Kong, you have created all sorts of havoc, but have been faithful in this journey. You shall be 'Buddha Victorious In Strife'.
BEN [*as Sun Wu Kong*]	[*in Mandarin*] Master, I'm now a Buddha like you. I should not wear the golden band on my head any more, so that if you choose to recite your spell, you could not plague me.
B [*as master*]	I have no spell to loosen the golden band. You will have to live with it, and still keep your image of a monkey.

SHIFT.

BEN	I have always liked Sun Wu Kong! I'm just like him, misunderstood and always alone. Even with all his powers of magic and creation, Sun Wu Kong could never escape the band on his head. It's with him forever, controlling him, hurting him. I have a band over my head too, and I can never take it off. I have to live with it, and learn to live with the pain. But I am different from Sun Wu Kong. In the story, he finishes his journey and attains enlightenment and freedom. I have

Journey to the West

just started on my journey -- where to? I don't know. Lu Shi Ren Zou Chu Lai De [*Mandarin*]. Once there was no path to begin with, but as we walk, a path will slowly be formed. The path may lead to nowhere, it may lead to somewhere, but at the end of it all; the path is mine -- because I walked on it, I created it.

Light fades.

THE END

Heart of the Land

DARREN MANNS

Darren Manns was born in 1978 in Roma in south west Queensland, Australia, where he works as a trainee dental assistant. He is also working to establish a community centre in the town to provide facilities for young Aboriginal and White people in the area.

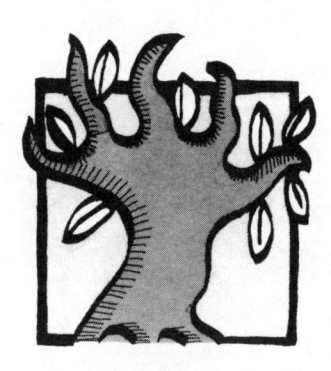

Heart of the Land

CHARACTERS

    NARRATOR
    COUNCIL MAN 1
    COUNCIL MAN 2

Scene One *is set in a traditional unspoilt bushland. Out of the darkness the didgeridoo is heard, gradually increasing in sound. Lights are made visible, moving around constantly in a slow formation. The lights represent the presence of the Dreamtime spirits of the land. Aboriginal singing and the sound of dance sticks is heard. The voice of an old man, an Aboriginal elder, who is playing the role of a spirit-like form, is then heard. He speaks a passage to give the audience a bit of knowledge about the culture of the Aborigine. Two European council workers then enter. They are in search of a dumping area. They realise that this area is significant but they don't care; it has no meaning for them. Council Man 2 is reading a newspaper. He stops Music and lights gradually fade away. This is the present, so lighting will be light blue.*

NARRATOR   For over 60,000 years before the white man took over this land, thinking it was empty, my people, the indigenous people, lived as one with their bush land, within an ordered community, a community with its own language, lifestyle and ideology deeply instilled in its people. The people and the land were as one.

COUNCIL MAN 1   Can't we just dump the rubbish here? It will save us a lot of time and money dumping here, rather than dumping at the town rubbish dump.

COUNCIL MAN 2   [*still looking at the paper*] I don't know. [*He looks up.*] Does anyone own this land?

He looks back at the newspaper.

COUNCIL MAN 1   [*sounds unsure, uses gestures and moves around while speaking*] Why? Should I know? Why should I care for that matter? Oh, hold on. [*Pause; sounds a little enthusiastic*] I think it's an Aboriginal burial site. Yeah that's right. It has been known as a sacred Aboriginal burial site since this town has been founded. [*He sounds uninterested; raises his hands and looks around.*] But I don't think anyone will care. Besides it doesn't look like a [*sarcastically*] sacred burial site - there's nothing here!

COUNCIL MAN 2   [*uncaring; still reading newspaper*] We may as well ...

COUNCIL MAN 1	[*sounds as if he has completed his job by finding a place to dump rubbish*] Fine. It's settled then.
COUNCIL MAN 2	[*offended*] Hey, take a look at this! Some bastard vandalised the town cemetary!
COUNCIL MAN 1	[*moving to look at the newspaper, he then moves away, shaking his head and sighing*] There is no respect these days.
COUNCIL MAN 2	[*folding up the paper; happy to leave*] Anyway, we've found a place to dump the rubbish.

Both leave, lights fade out.

Scene Two

In a traditional setting, Aboriginals act out how the most sacred part of the land came to be. The Narrator takes the audience back to the past, to show how important the burial site is. It is the past, therefore lighting will be red ochre.

NARRATOR	[*in darkness*] In the time of the beginning, burial sites had to be established in every tribe, for every tribe's person. The burial site was the doorway for the person's spirit to enter the time of dreaming.

The didgeridoo is heard. Lights focus on totem poles in the background.

> This is how the Mandandanji burial site was born. This is how the doorway to the time of dreaming came to be. Ever since time began, burial sites were known to be very spiritual - with importance - and most of all great significance. The area had to be unique compared to the rest of land.

Music stops. Lights from all areas of the stage flicker on and off. The colour is white.

> In the clan Ongarri, the ruler knew his time was coming to an end. As the clan was travelling in search of a burial site and camping area [*lights stop flickering, but focus on the background area, where a tree in the shape of a hand is visible*] a tree was noticed, standing alone. It was in the shape of a hand. The general tribespeople could not go near any part of the tree and surrounding area. They were forced away by an invisible force field. Only the Kiddichi man and the elders of the tribe were 'excepted' and could associate with this certain area. The Elder, wise as he was, knew by the guidance of the dreaming spirits that this is where his bones, alongside his symbolic belongings, would be grasped for the rest of eternity. The Elder then instructed that this was to be the burial site for the Mandandanji tribe.

Heart of the Land

From then on, this became the 'Heart of the Land'.

Music starts up, consisting of singing, the didgeridoo and the dance sticks.

A special ceremony was then held by the Kiddichi man. This was necessary for the doorway to the time of dreaming to be opened, to let the spirit of the tribesperson enter the time of dreaming. It was also necessary to make it 'official', to make sure that this burial site would always be the 'Heart of the Land'. Also, from this day forward, everyone would respect the most sacred and spiritual area of the whole tribe.

Lights fade out, music continues to play for twenty seconds, and then fades out.

Scene Three

The clan moves to the other side of the creek and sets up camp. The members of the clan recommence their daily lives. When the lights come up, the clan is spread around the stage miming the hunting, the gathering, the ceremonies and the telling of dreamtime stories. It is set in the past.

NARRATOR The people of the Ongarri clan then set up on the other side of the creek. The people of the land recommenced their daily lives which included hunting, [*pause*] gathering, [*pause*] dancing, [*pause*] ceremonies [*pause*] and the telling of dreamtime stories.

Lights fade out. One light focuses on an Elder and the children, in which a dreamtime story will be told. The Elder will mime the telling of the dreamtime story, while on the opposite side of the stage, dancers will act and dance out the story. They will dance in an area of different light. This will create a hologram effect for the audience.

So that the next generation would remember this day, a special dreamtime story was told of how the beautiful Brolga came to be.

Music starts and lights come up. The story-teller uses gestures whilst speaking. Light will show a defined circle. To see Brolga, already on centre stage right, the colour will a soft blue light.

In the time of the dreaming, there was a beautiful girl called Brolga. She was loved by all the members of the tribe because she was kind and always shared with others. She was most of all loved and admired for the way she danced.

Brolga imitates the actions being said.

Everyone watched her as she picked berries, yams from the ground, and mud mussels from the billabong. Her magical movements were copied by the tribe as they danced the corroboree around the fire at night.

Actors dance around in a circle.

All the men wanted Brolga for their wife.

Men move close to Brolga; Brolga moves away.

But Brolga said she belonged to the tribe and not to one man. One day, when Brolga was out collecting berries, Gilligil, who really wanted to marry Brolga, watched her from behind the bushes. Brolga went on dancing, picking berries from all over the bush.

Both actors act out what is being said.

Gilligil jumped out from behind the bushes and told Brolga of his love for her. Brolga pushed him away. In his rage he said, 'If I can't have you, then no-one will!'

Gilligil picks up a stone and hits her on the head.

With that he picked up a stone and struck Brolga on the head.
Gilligil, in shame, ran into the bushes and was never seen again.

The tribe found Brolga lying dead on the ground, with blood on top of her head. They danced around her, asking the dreamtime spirits to save their special dancer. In the midst of the dancers, Brolga rose anew.

The music and the atmosphere change. Hologrammic area becomes misty. Lighting becomes dull, to create an eerie feeling.

She had become a beautiful white bird. The tribe knew it was her because she danced in the same magical way in which their former Brolga had.

Lights fade out on the storyteller and children. Tribespeople disappear, leaving Brolga continuing to dance solo.

Even today, Brolga continues to dance in her special and magical ways, and on top of the bird's head still remain the red marks where Gilligil hit beautiful Brolga.

Lights and music slowly fade out.

This story has been passed down from generation to generation, showing the importance of the day the burial site was formed. It shows the importance of why we must always fight to keep the burial sites significant, to keep the 'Heart of the Land' beating forever.

Scene Four

The past. The burial site area. Lights come up to reveal the Kiddichi man already on stage. Lighting is red ochre.

NARRATOR   This is how the first meeting of the Aboriginal and the European turned out to be.
One day the Kiddichi man was watching over the burial site, making sure the dreaming spirits were with the land. At that point, the first white man was travelling in the area exploring, in wonder at how much this land had to offer his people. At that point, he started to trespass on the sacred burial site. Tribal law has it that no-one, except the Kiddichi man and the Elders of the tribe, could enter and associate with the burial site. The Kiddichi man did not know who, or what, or where this stranger with white skin had come from.

Kiddichi man moves slowly towards the explorer and his men.

The Kiddichi man called for the warriors.

The explorer gives command to shoot.

The explorer and his men, frightened and confused, raised a stick and then, followed by a loud bang, the Kiddichi man fell to the ground, never to rise again.

Scene Five

The present day, in the same area of the burial site. Lights come up to reveal a massive dump where the Mandandanji tribe's burial site used to be. Council workers dump rubbish throughout the following scene.

NARRATOR   The white man disappeared ... but not for long. Australia's history is so significant to an understanding of Aboriginal culture and heritage, that it must not be desecrated. It must not be used as a dump. Since the white man came to this land, the culture of the Aborigine has been buried under their alien culture.

At this point, the narrator's voice becomes weak, getting softer because of the talking about the white man and what he has done to the culture of the Aborigine.

> The burial site has never been used again. No-one recognised it as being the most sacred, spiritual and important area of the whole tribe.
> The 'Heart of the Land' was never seen as important and significant, just like many other sacred sites all over Australia.

The Narrator's voice becomes very weak. He strains to force the words out.

> There is no simple answer.
> The past is the past,
> so start healing.
> Don't need to have black skin to be Aboriginal,
> it's what's in the heart that matters.
> Hold onto your history through what is left.
> Keep the heart strong,
> With every beat.
> Clean up your act,
> or the culture of the Aborigine will be buried, and will fade away forever, forever, forever, forever . . .

The voice of the Narrator slowly fades away as it echoes. Council workers dumping rubbish look up to notice that the voice is gone. A look of shame is on their faces. They act as if they did not know, they act as if it is not their fault. Lights slowly fade out after ten seconds.

THE END

On the Island

PAWEL MARCIN NOWAK

Pawel Marcin Nowak was born in 1977 in Poland and is a secondary school student in Kielce. In 1988 and 1992 he was a prizewinner in Poland's playwrighting competition 'Looking for the Polish Shakespeare'. He has also won poetry prizes and in 1993 a collection of his poems was published in Warsaw.

CHARACTERS

    THE YOUNG CASTAWAY
    THE OLD CASTAWAY

SETTING

No decorations. A circle of light on the place where the castaways sit.

Scene One

The Old Castaway looks at the Young one, who is unconscious, but starts to wake up. The Old Castaway plays chess with himself.

YOUNG CASTAWAY	Where... Where am I!?!
OLD CASTAWAY	Here...
YOUNG CASTAWAY	Yes...
OLD CASTAWAY	Nice of you to agree with me.
YOUNG CASTAWAY	Yes... What... What has happened?
OLD CASTAWAY	Sorry, I can't tell you. I was asleep when you came here.
YOUNG CASTAWAY	But... What could have happened?!
OLD CASTAWAY	Well, if you were travelling on a ship...
YOUNG CASTAWAY	Yes! I remember that!
OLD CASTAWAY	That lets me eliminate the other hypothesis...
YOUNG CASTAWAY	And what was that?
OLD CASTAWAY	I just thought you might be Icarus.
YOUNG CASTAWAY	No.

On the Island

OLD CASTAWAY	But I knew it was rather impossible.
YOUNG CASTAWAY	But what could have happened to my ship?
OLD CASTAWAY	Well... I suppose that it has been the same sort of thing that happened to mine some time ago.
YOUNG CASTAWAY	And what was that?
OLD CASTAWAY	Sorry, I can't tell you either. I was asleep, unconscious or something like that, I don't remember now.
YOUNG CASTAWAY	But I want to know what has happened!
OLD CASTAWAY	OK, OK! Let me just suggest to you one way of finding the solution to this problem.
YOUNG CASTAWAY	What do you mean?
OLD CASTAWAY	Thinking about it.
YOUNG CASTAWAY	Do you think my ship could have got wrecked?
OLD CASTAWAY	No! I would rather say that you are a dead sailor who was thrown into the ocean to be buried there.
YOUNG CASTAWAY	[*after a moment of silence*] So I am a shipwrecked person now?
OLD CASTAWAY	Castaway is the other word for it.
YOUNG CASTAWAY	Are you ... Are we the only people on this island?
OLD CASTAWAY	Well, it is crowded enough here.
YOUNG CASTAWAY	Yes, you are right ... is there at least something to eat here?
OLD CASTAWAY	Well, now, when you came ... Don't be afraid, I was joking.
YOUNG CASTAWAY	So is there something to eat -- apart from me and you?
OLD CASTAWAY	Think a while. Do I look like a ghost?
YOUNG CASTAWAY	No ... Yes, you have to eat something ...
OLD CASTAWAY	There are the palms.

YOUNG CASTAWAY	Only that?
OLD CASTAWAY	There were enough coconuts for me and there will be enough of them for both of us.
YOUNG CASTAWAY	Well, don't think I am going to stay here long.
OLD CASTAWAY	So what are you going to do?
YOUNG CASTAWAY	What? Well, I am going to escape, to be rescued!
OLD CASTAWAY	Interesting. How?
YOUNG CASTAWAY	I can swim ...
OLD CASTAWAY	Two thousand miles with five sharks on every yard?
YOUNG CASTAWAY	Well ... I know; I will build a raft!
OLD CASTAWAY	There are three palms here, young man.
YOUNG CASTAWAY	Enough.
OLD CASTAWAY	Maybe, but there is a little problem.
YOUNG CASTAWAY	What problem?
OLD CASTAWAY	No palms - no coconuts.
YOUNG CASTAWAY	And what are the coconuts for, if I ... if we leave this island?
OLD CASTAWAY	Oh, no! Don't try to count on me!
YOUNG CASTAWAY	There will be enough space on the raft for both of us!
OLD CASTAWAY	There will be enough space. But we would drown after two miles or so.
YOUNG CASTAWAY	But we've got to do something! I can't spend the rest of my life here! I am young!
OLD CASTAWAY	I was young, too, when I had to start living here.
YOUNG CASTAWAY	And you didn't try to do anything?

OLD CASTAWAY	Of course I did.
YOUNG CASTAWAY	And what?
OLD CASTAWAY	And nothing.
YOUNG CASTAWAY	But what did you do?
OLD CASTAWAY	I made a raft. I have used four palms to build it. I was lucky to get back here, before the whole construction went to pieces.
YOUNG CASTAWAY	I will find another solution. You will see. I can promise you that in a short time we will be among people again!
OLD CASTAWAY	Yhm. And if I don't want to come back to people?
YOUNG CASTAWAY	Of course you want. It is obvious.
OLD CASTAWAY	Not for me.

Blackout.

Scene Two

Both castaways play chess.

YOUNG CASTAWAY	You are a good player.
OLD CASTAWAY	Years of practice.
YOUNG CASTAWAY	I bet you could beat the world champion.
OLD CASTAWAY	You would have to bring him here to check it.
YOUNG CASTAWAY	Or to get you out of here.
OLD CASTAWAY	Yhm.
YOUNG CASTAWAY	OK, finish it faster, please. Because of playing I forgot to observe the sea.
OLD CASTAWAY	You are still thinking how to get out of here?
YOUNG CASTAWAY	And you aren't?

OLD CASTAWAY	Checkmate.
YOUNG CASTAWAY	Thank you.
OLD CASTAWAY	Come back, we will play again.
YOUNG CASTAWAY	Are you not bored with chess?
OLD CASTAWAY	What else could I do here?
YOUNG CASTAWAY	And that is why I want to get back to the world.
OLD CASTAWAY	Just another way of wasting time, believe me.
YOUNG CASTAWAY	There must be a ship passing by, at least sometimes!
OLD CASTAWAY	So why didn't I leave this island so far?
YOUNG CASTAWAY	You must have not noticed them or they must have not noticed you.
OLD CASTAWAY	Oh, how stupid you are ...
YOUNG CASTAWAY	I don't see any other explanation.
OLD CASTAWAY	And what if I had occasions and I didn't use them.
YOUNG CASTAWAY	I don't believe you.
OLD CASTAWAY	Why?
YOUNG CASTAWAY	You are not mad.
OLD CASTAWAY	You think I'd have to be mad to want to stay here?
YOUNG CASTAWAY	Of course.
OLD CASTAWAY	You still know very little about being a castaway!
YOUNG CASTAWAY	I would never believe that someone would like to stay here alone for years! Maybe if he was mad, but you are not mad!
OLD CASTAWAY	What if I like such a life?

On the Island

YOUNG CASTAWAY	And what life is it? Playing chess over and over again and eating these damned coconuts?! I can't look at them any more!
OLD CASTAWAY	Will you eat them with your eyes closed or will there be more left for me?
YOUNG CASTAWAY	It was a sort of metaphor.
OLD CASTAWAY	Are you going to play again?
YOUNG CASTAWAY	I will observe the sea for some more time.
OLD CASTAWAY	As you want.
YOUNG CASTAWAY	Or wait. I will play.

Blackout.

Scene Three

Castaways play chess. A lot of time has passed.

OLD CASTAWAY	What would you do if you saw a ship now?
YOUNG CASTAWAY	I would get up as fast as possible, shout, scream and wave my hands. I would do everything to be noticed. Or I should rather say: we would do everything to be noticed.
OLD CASTAWAY	I've told you many times I wouldn't make a single move.
YOUNG CASTAWAY	I've told you many times I don't believe you.
OLD CASTAWAY	So you say you would scream, wave your hands and perhaps your shirt, to make them notice you?
YOUNG CASTAWAY	We would, to make them notice us.
OLD CASTAWAY	So why don't you do anything when there is a big, beautiful ship behind you?
YOUNG CASTAWAY	Yhm.
OLD CASTAWAY	Just turn to check it.
YOUNG CASTAWAY	Stupid joke.

OLD CASTAWAY	It is not a joke.
YOUNG CASTAWAY	Yhm. You had better concentrate on playing.
OLD CASTAWAY	Your choice.
YOUNG CASTAWAY	Do you really think I would not recognise the day of salvation?
OLD CASTAWAY	You don't want to recognise it.
YOUNG CASTAWAY	Stop that. Play.
OLD CASTAWAY	Just turn if you don't believe me.
YOUNG CASTAWAY	No.
OLD CASTAWAY	Just turn.
YOUNG CASTAWAY	Play.
OLD CASTAWAY	There is really a ship there.
YOUNG CASTAWAY	Play.
OLD CASTAWAY	I can shout instead of you.
YOUNG CASTAWAY	Your king is in danger.
OLD CASTAWAY	I knew it would be like that. It is gone. They won't hear us ... you ... now.
YOUNG CASTAWAY	[*turning*] You thought that cloud there was a ship?
OLD CASTAWAY	It was a ship.
YOUNG CASTAWAY	Checkmate. Do you want a new game?
OLD CASTAWAY	And what else can I do?

THE END

Ji-Da (The Bird)

AMY VANESSA ROBERTS

Amy Vanessa Roberts was born in Western Australia in 1978. She is a dance graduate from the Graduate College of Dance in Perth where she studied classical, contemporary, character and Spanish dance, and has performed in many productions as a dancer and actor. Since 1992 she has also been writing plays.

CHARACTERS

> VOICE
> YOUNG ABORIGINAL MAN / JI-DA
> ODESSA, *Aboriginal girl about 10 years of age*
> BRANDON, *Odessa's brother, age 12*
> MISS JONES, *School teacher*
> MOR, *Mother of Odessa and Brandon*
> FAR, *Father of Odessa and Brandon*
> MANYOOWA (1), *Grandmother of Odessa and Brandon*
> MANYOOWA (2), *Grandmother of Odessa and Brandon*
> WARDA KUDUK, *Grandfather of Odessa and Brandon*
> DREAMTIME ELDERS *(five)*
> ABORIGINAL ADULTS *(five male, five female)*
> ABORIGINAL CHILDREN *(five male, five female), ages 5-14*
> SHERRY, *Aboriginal girl, age 10*
> JOHN, *Aboriginal boy, age 14*
> ABORIGINAL BOYS *(three) ages 12-14*

SETTING

The play takes place with the background of a rugged mountain range.

Prelude

Background of rugged mountain range. Young Aboriginal Man is sitting next to a campfire. He is dressed in baggy pants, long-sleeved shirt and wears a beanie hat on his head. His feet are bare.

YOUNG MAN What's happening? The fire is changing colour! [*His hands go around the flames of the fire.*] The fire is cold. [*He reaches to place a log onto the fire. A voice comes out of the fire.*]

Softly in the background Aboriginal music can be heard.

VOICE From past to present the Dreamtime must continue. You, being a part of this, will be sent to teach your people. Through the eyes of a bird you will be able to watch. Through your song you will exert influence. Your presence is itself an almost magical influence on events and people. Your time now is in the settlement of the Quamera's. It is no accident that you are to be there. There are many things your ancestors are concerned about. You are to be a spiritual emissary sent to change people's mistakes.

YOUNG MAN Why are you saying this to me? What do I have to do with this? [*Fire goes out; a white light appears upstage right; Young Man gets up and walks toward the light.*] Where's that light coming from? I feel weird, it is pulling me toward it! [*He tries to pull away from the light.*] I can't seem to get myself away from it! [*He stands in the light then follows it offstage.*]

Act One, Scene One

The Dreamtime. Young Man is standing centre stage. He is surrounded by coloured light as if he is in the campfire. Five Dreamtime Elders dance around him chanting. In the background slides of animals, reptiles, birds and rock drawings are flashed onto a screen. While the Elders dance around him the Young Man removes his clothing to reveal his bird-self. The bird is a white egret. As he changes the Voice translates the chanting of the Elders.

VOICE The children of the next generation are ruining their lives inhaling poisons. Their spirits are slowly dying, wasting away. So, that is why you are here. You are being sent from the Dreamtime to help the people of the Quamera.

BIRD This is weird! I've got to get out of here!

Scene Two

Shanty group of houses. Background of rugged mountain ranges. Tree is in the foreground. The bird is in the tree. Odessa is sitting under the tree leaning against the trunk. She is writing in a diary.

ODESSA [*speaking as she writes*] Dear diary, Miss Jones, our teacher, says we should write in our diary every day. But it makes me sad to write. I wish my family would stop fighting and be happy like they were when I was little. My family is broken up into little pieces. Dad is drinking again. He has not been able to get work. He is a good worker but the farms around here are having it tough, so they are not putting anyone on. Mum gets depressed, she has diabetes; the health worker says she needs to eat better than she does. I worry about Brandon; he is going with other boys to the *kap wari* [water hole] to sniff glue. I don't know what to do.

Odessa starts to weep and drops her head to her knees. The diary falls to the ground.

JI-DA [*speaking from perch in tree*] This is the reason I'm here! This is what the Elders were talking about. This is the girl... A child of the Quamera tribe. How can I get her attention? She seems so involved in her family problems. [*Ji-Da tilts his head to one side, notices the dropped diary, jumps down from his* perch and grabs the diary; he reads the first page of the diary.] So that's her name ... Odessa.

He turns, and flies off.

ODESSA [*lifting her head in time to see bird taking off with her diary.*] Hey you! You *kat wara ji-da* [stupid bird], give me back my diary. Give it back to me now! [*Odessa runs off after the bird, shouting*] Kat wara ji-da! Kat wara ji-da!

Act Two, Scene One

Quamera Settlement School. A one room, one teacher school for primary and secondary students. Miss Jones is at her desk preparing lessons for the day. The school playground has a basketball ring and several children are playing basketball. Ji-Da enters and runs amongst the children. Odessa enters and chases Ji-Da. Finally Ji-Da drops the diary near the entrance to the classroom.

ODESSA Why did you take my diary, you *kat wara ji-da*? I hope you have not mucked it up, or Miss Jones will tell me off!

JI-DA [*perched in a tree in the schoolyard.*] I need your diary so I can help you. I cannot tell you who I am, but I have been sent to help the children of the Quamera of this generation to understand that they are slowly dying and wasting away. Unless they stop poisoning themselves and their spirits, there will be no more Quamera. In time it will be revealed to you how you and your family can once again be happy.

The school bell rings. Odessa turns away from Ji-Da and joins the other children as they line up and enter school. The children take their seats.

MISS JONES Good Morning children. [*Children reply 'Good Morning Miss Jones'.*] What a beautiful day it is today. Have you brought your diaries? [*Children reach for diaries on top of their desks, hands go up. Miss Jones looks around the class.*] O.K. John, let's hear from you. What did you write about?

JOHN [*Stands and reads from diary.*] Sunday, me and Dad went to Sunshine Gorge. We went to hunt kangaroo. We saw some big Greys and Dad was able to get one. We brought it back and Mum cooked it and all the family came and ate it.

He sits down.

MISS JONES	Thank you John. How about you Sherry? What have you written?
SHERRY	[*stands and reads*] Saturday we collected dried grasses and bark and Manyoowa showed us girls how to make baskets. She says we might be able to sell them at the co-op in town. I hope we can 'cause I would like to buy some new tapes 'cause me old ones are getting worn out.
MISS JONES	Thank you Sherry. Perhaps you could bring along one of your baskets for all the class to see. [*Sherry smiles as she sits down.*] Thank you John and Sherry for sharing with us your very interesting diary entries. We do not have time for any more today, as we must get along with our history lesson. Remember we talked about the world's great explorers and how they sailed around the world discovering new lands? Now, who can tell me the name of the famous explorer who discovered Australia?

Some children raise their hands, Brandon is one of them.

	Yes, Brandon?
BRANDON	My Dad says it was not that Captain Cook fella you told us about. He says we Aborigines found Australia at the beginning of time when the white fellas still lived in their caves. I reckon it's pretty crook the way Captain Cook always gets a mention as the fella who discovered Australia!
MISS JONES	Brandon, that is enough! I will not tolerate cheekiness in this classroom. [*The children begin to snigger.*] Quiet children! Captain James Cook was among the first English explorers to discover the east coast of Australia. If you turn to Page 26 in your history book, you can read an entry from Captain Cook's Ship's Log. Can anyone tell me what a Ship's Log is? [*Odessa raises her hand.*] Yes Odessa?
ODESSA	It's the ship's diary.
MISS JONES	Good! That's right, it is the ship's diary. Now I want you to draw in exercise books, a picture of Captain Cook as he discovers Australia.
BRANDON	[*talks loudly to a friend*] Hey, this Captain Cook stuff is stupid!

Miss Jones is about to say something to him when Odessa and Brandon's Father bursts into the classroom. He is drunk.

FAR	[*he staggers and his voice is slurred.*] Odessa! Odessa! Where are you girl?

Odessa tries to hide under her desk. Far looks around the classroom, spots Odessa and staggers toward her. He makes a grab at her, pulls her out from under the desk and struggles with her.

ODESSA No Dad, no! Leave me alone.

Far drags Odessa to the door. Miss Jones runs to help Odessa.

MISS JONES Leave her alone and leave this classroom! Odessa, please go back to your desk while I talk to your Father outside. [*Miss Jones places herself between Odessa and her Father. She faces Far.*] I have told you to leave. I will speak to you outside.

Far goes to strike Odessa. He misses and hits Miss Jones. She is knocked out. Far staggers out into the playground. Odessa follows him. Some of the children gather around Miss Jones and attempt to revive her. Ji-Da has been a silent observer from his perch. As Far staggers into the playground, Ji-Da leaves his perch and chases him. He attacks him. Far falls to the ground on his knees. Ji-Da stands in front of him and lets out a song. Pre-recorded music is played.

JI-DA I bring you a message from your ancestors! You need to change your ways. You must return to the spiritual ways of your Father and his Father before him. You are of a special people chosen to be the keepers of the Dreaming, and without you the Spirit of the Dreamtime will wither and die with you... and your children and their children will never learn of their heritage.

FAR [*Far looks at Ji-Da, cries for a few moments and breaks down.*] Bird, I do not know who you are, but you have helped me. I know what I must do for my children.

ODESSA [*Calling to Ji-Da, as he goes.*] Thank you, Thank you Ji-Da!

Scene Two

At the kap wari [water hole] Brandon and three other boys are about to sniff a large pot of glue. Ji-Da is bathing himself while watching the boys.

BOY ONE Hey Brandon, your Dad caused a stir in class today. Bet the cops will be around at your place tonight!

BOY TWO Yeah, reckon they'll haul him off to the lockup!

BOY THREE Come on, let's get sniffing right away. I've been waiting all day for this. I love the way it makes me feel. I feel no pain. It's good.

BOY TWO   Yeah! Guess I got lucky when I broke into the school storeroom last night. This is real *moodity* [solid]. Miss Jones didn't even notice it was gone.

BRANDON   Look, I don't think we should sniff this stuff!

BOY ONE   What, you chicken or something?

He shoves Brandon in the chest while making chicken noises.

BRANDON   No! I'm not. It's just that the health worker was talking to Mum. You know she comes to check on her diabetes. She told her my cousin Jason is *kaat warabiny* [going mad] from sniffing glue. He's got brain damage and he has to live in a home for brain-damaged kids.

A whistle is heard. The boys turn to see Odessa entering.

ODESSA   Brandon! Brandon! Where are you?

Ji-Da suddenly dashes over and grabs the pot of glue. He runs to the water hole and throws the pot. A splash can be heard. All are watching the Bird. The three boys shake angry fists at the Bird.

BRANDON   Thank you Bird. [*Ji-Da lets out his song. Pre-recorded music plays.*] Thanks Ji-Da... I will never sniff glue again! Come on Odessa, I'll race you home.

Brandon and Odessa run off.

Act Three, Scene One

Ji-Da is sitting in a tree with rugged mountain ranges in background.

JI-DA   Where is she? She is never late. I wonder what is keeping her? I heard loud angry noises coming from the Quamera last night. I hope Odessa and Brandon are alright. I wonder where she can be? I think I will check out the school. She might be there.

Blackout.

Scene Two

The schoolyard and the classroom. Ji-Da is perched up in the tree. Miss Jones and Odessa's Mother are in the playground. The school children are lined up ready to enter class.

MISS JONES   You're Odessa and Brandon's Mother aren't you? It's nice to be able to meet you. Is there a problem with Odessa or Brandon?

MOR   Brandon told me that you said he was cheeky to you when he tried to tell you that Captain Cook was not the first to discover Australia. How come you can't teach him about Aboriginals who were explorers long before you *wadjella* [white people] got here?

MISS JONES   Well, I must use the history books in our curriculum and they do not tell about any Aboriginal explorers and I have never read or heard of any. If I don't stick to the curriculum I will be in trouble with Head Office.

MOR   I don't care about any curriculum or whatever you call it. I am sick and tired of a racist *janger yorger* [white woman] teaching my children about Captain Cook and all that *wadjella* stuff, as if Aborigines never belonged here. I want my children to be proud of being Aboriginal and of their heritage. Why can't you teach them that we were here as owners of the land since time began, long before Captain Cook or any other whitefellas.

MISS JONES   I'm sorry you feel that way. I do care about the children I teach. I want them to be proud of their culture and their heritage. Can you tell me what I can do to help them?

Mother hangs her head and stares at the ground. She turns and walks off. Miss Jones walks over to the waiting children.

MISS JONES   Hurry up children, we are late already. [*Children enter classroom and sit at their desks. Miss Jones passes out readers to children.*] Today children I have something I must attend to. Please read quietly the book I have given you. If you need me just come quietly to my desk. Please do not disturb the other children in class.

Miss Jones sits at her desk with a pen and notebook. Ji-Da comes down from his perch and sits near her desk. She becomes aware of his presence.

     Oh, what a beautiful bird you are. I wonder why you have been sitting in the school ground. Why have you come here?

Ji-Da lifts his head and gives out his song. Pre-recorded music is heard.

     Thank you bird! You have given me an idea.

Ji-Da looks over Miss Jones' shoulder as she writes. Odessa waves to Ji-Da from her desk. Ji-Da leaves classroom.

Scene Three

Bird is perched in tree with rugged mountains in background.

JI-DA I feel that today is the day when everything I was sent for will be revealed. I can hardly wait to see what will take place.

Odessa and Brandon enter and approach the tree.

BRANDON Ji-Da, Ji-Da, are you there? Come on, it's time to go to school!

ODESSA Ji-Da, we do not want to be late. Come on!

Ji-Da comes down from his tree and follows Odessa and Brandon. Blackout.

Scene Four

The schoolyard class scene. The children are at their desks and are saying their times tables.

CHILDREN [*not in unison*] Ten tens are one hundred, eleven tens are one hundred and ten, twelve tens are one hundred and twenty.

MISS JONES Thank you children. You are coming along beautifully and I am so proud of you. Today we are going to have a special treat. There will be no more lessons today. I have a surprise for you. John, will you have all the boys line up behind you and Sherry, could you take all the girls [*The children jostle for places*]. Good. Now we are are ready for our surprise. It is not far from here. John and Sherry, could you please lead the others around to the back of the school.

Children follow John and Sherry out; Miss Jones is standing alone in the classroom

Well, I hope this works. I do so want to help the children

She goes.

Scene Five

A group of Aboriginal adults are gathered around a campfire. Odessa's parents are there along with Manyoowa One and Two and Warda Kaduk. The group is dressed in the traditional way. Piles of boomerangs, didgeridoo and clapping sticks are on the ground. Some of the group are working at bark painting and basket weaving. The children enter. Odessa sees Manyoowa and runs to her. Brandon sees Warda Kaduk and he goes to him. The other children gather around the adults. Ji-Da enters and comes to sit by Warda Kaduk. Miss Jones enters and approaches the Elders near the campfire.

MISS JONES   Thank you everyone for coming. It is wonderful to have you come today. I have nothing further to say, except to say to the children please enjoy yourself at this corroboree that the elders of the Quamera tribe have planned for you.

Miss Jones goes and sits with a group of women.

WARDA KADUK   We are happy Miss Jones invited us to come be with you today. But we need your help to make this corroboree.

Clapping sticks are handed to the girls. Boomerangs and didgeridoo to the boys. The Elders begin to sing; the children join in with clapping sticks, etc. Brandon and John have solos with the didgeridoo. Some younger boys try, with little success, to copy them. The singing dies down. Odessa turns to Manyoowa One.

ODESSA   Manyoowa, will you tell us a story from the Dreamtime?

MANYOOWA ONE   Alright Granddaughter. I will tell you about Unwarra's Web of Death. Long ago we Quamera had our own laws long before the *wadjella* came. Our laws were strong and were not to be broken. To do so was to have harsh punishment. Unwara, the spiderman, lived near a lake. He had to look after his two nephews Nali and Balinga. Unwara was a very powerful medicine man... Do you want to hear more?

CHILDREN   Yes Manyoowa.

MANYOOWA ONE   Well, the nephews fell in love with two sisters from another tribe. They asked the sisters to come live with them even though this was against the tribal law. Unwara and the tribal Elders were angry. The next day Unwara sent his nephews off to do some hunting. He sent the sisters to gather yams and grass seeds. As soon as the nephews were out of sight he turned the sisters into *widji* [emu] and sent them to a *kap wari*. Soon the nephews returned empty handed from the hunt. Unwara told them 'be quick, I saw two widji down by the kap wari'. Nali and Balinga stalked the widji. They were easy to spear and catch. This was because the sisters recognised their lovers and made no

Ji-Da

attempt to run away. When the nephews brought the dead widji back to camp their uncle laughed scornfully at them. He told them they had killed the girls they loved so much... Do you want to know more?

CHILDREN   Yes!

MANYOOWA ONE   Because they had disobeyed the tribal law they were banished from their tribe never to see the land of their birth again.

On completion of the story, some men and a few of the boys do the Emu Dance. Soon all the men and boys are dancing. As the dance finishes Odessa turns to Manyoowa Two.

ODESSA   Manyoowa, please tell me my favourite story about how Kuljak was once a white swan, not black.

MANYOOWA TWO   Long ago in the Dreamtime, there were only swans who were white. This was to be until one fateful day when Kuljak accidentally landed on the lagoon that belonged to *Wald-ja* [Eagle hawk]. Wald-ja was angry that Kuljak and his friends had trespassed on his property, and he and his friends began to attack them. Poor Kuljak, the attack was so brutal that it tore out most of his feathers and those of the other swans. Wald-ja and the rest of the eagle hawks then picked up the battered swans, and carried them far into the desert to die. Do you know what happened?

ODESSA   Yes, but you tell us.

MANYOOWA TWO   Unprotected by the scorching sun by day and the bitter cold by night, Kuljak lay in pain and agony. One day he and his friends heard a call. Looking up they saw *Wardang* [black crow] and his friends flying above them. Wardang felt such pity for Kuljak. He plucked some black feathers from his body, and his crow friends did the same. They let the feathers fall on the swans. Wardang then cried out to Kuljak, 'Wald-ja is our enemy too. Our feathers will protect you until you have grown strong again.'
As time went by the swans did grow stronger. They flew to the land south of the Quamera now known as the Southwest of Western Australia. Today Kuljak and his swan friends are no longer white. Black covers most of their body except for a few white feathers on their wing tips. Their beaks are red as a constant reminder that Wald-ja is still their enemy.

Music begins to play. The men and boys get up to dance; the girls and women join them in the dance that tells the story of Kuljak, Wald-ja and Wardong. As the dance concludes, the lights dim as if sunset is about to take place.

Finale

Everyone is gathered around the campfire. Ji-Da sits next to Warda Kaduk. A new chant begins. Ji-Da gets up, makes some dance steps, then pauses.

JI-DA I know this song. It is familiar to me [*He does some dance steps*] Ah! Yes, it is my song, the song of Ji-Da.

Warda Kaduk and Brandon join Ji-Da in the dance. As the dance finishes, Brandon sits down. Warda Kaduk approaches Ji-Da and stares him in the eyes. He begins to softly chant while stamping his feet. He circles Ji-Da, who turns with him as they keep eye contact. When the chant is ended, Warda Kaduk sits down. Ji-Da is left standing alone. During the chanting and circling, all leave except Brandon and Odessa, who stay with Warda Kaduk and Ji-Da.

JI-DA I feel strange. I am being pulled into the campfire.

Warda Kaduk begins to chant again while sitting. A series of lights resembling a flickering campfire surround Ji-Da.

I feel the Dreamtime Elders calling me. Goodbye Odessa! Goodbye Brandon! It is time for me to go. You are two wonderful children with beautiful spirits. Do all you can to protect them.

The bird song is heard, pre-recorded music plays.

BRANDON & ODESSA Bye Ji-Da, bye! We will never forget you!

As a mist appears Odessa, Brandon and Warda Kaduk leave. As the mist clears, the Deamtime Elders appear and begin to circle Ji-Da who is in the centre. They are chanting and Ji-Da is dressing back into the clothes of the Young Aboriginal Man. As he dresses the Voice translates the chants of the Dreamtime Elders.

VOICE Your work is done. You have done well. The children of the Quamera will remember you always and will try to protect their spirits from poisons. They now understand the importance of the spiritual self. From past to present the Dreamtime must continue.

A white light appears. Young Aboriginal Man goes to it. He follows its crying and goes.

YOUNG ABORIGINAL MAN	Warda Kaduk, Odessa's Grandfather; he knew!

Song of Ji-Da is heard; pre-recorded music plays. Blackout.

THE END

GLOSSARY

NYOONGAH	ENGLISH
Boomerang	Hunting weapon carved from curved wood; used as musical instrument by tapping two together
Corroboree	Tribal gathering; ceremonial meeting
Didgeridoo	Musical instrument made from hollow tree limb; only played by males
Janger yorger	White woman
Ji-Da	Bird
Kap wari	Waterhole
Kat wara	Stupid
Kaat warabiny	Going mad
Kuljak	Black swan
Manyoowa	Grandmother
Moodity	Solid (good/reliable)
Wadjella	Europeans
Wald-ja	Eaglehawk
Wardang	Black crow
Warda Kaduk	Man of renown
Widji	Emu

Lovepuke

DUNCAN SARKIES

Duncan Sarkies was born in New Zealand in 1970 and lives in Dunedin. He began writing plays at the age of ten and studied with playwright Roger Hall at Otago University. He has worked as a director, actor and comic performer. In 1993 in Wellington, *Lovepuke* won the 'Best of the Fringe Festival' award.

Lovepuke

CHARACTERS

GLEN
HERMIONE
IVAN
JANICE
KEVIN
LOUISE
MARISSA
NATHAN

SETTING

An empty stage except for a ladder at the back and seven chairs in a line. At the top of the ladder hang large sheets of cardboard denoting the name of each scene. Each time the play moves on to a new scene, the character Glen cuts off the piece of string holding the currently-shown sheet, revealing the title of the new scene on the cardboard behind it. (In this book, scene titles are in **bold** type.) At the end of the play, there will be just one sheet of cardboard remaining, the rest will have dropped to the floor. In addition, each character holds a series of words on cardboard signs, which are thrown down after being spoken. (In this book, these words/signs are printed in capital letters e.g: ARGUMENT). No extra props are necessary - when a camera is required all that is needed is a sign saying CAMERA. At the end the stage will be littered with cardboard.

As the play begins, six of the seven chairs are empty. Hermione sits, intensely focused at a point at the side of the stage. She remains semi-frozen in this way until she first speaks. Glen stands near the top of the ladder with a pair of scissors. When he cuts down the LOVEPUKE sign, the play begins.

The Bit after the End

Kevin and Louise enter and stand in front of their seats.

GLEN Well?

Pause.

LOUISE Um ...

In this sequence people say the words as well as throw away the bits of cardboard.

SEX. ARGUMENT. ARGUMENT. MAKE UP. SEX. ARGUMENT. ARGUMENT. Um ...
ARGUMENT. ARGUMENT. BREAK UP. Um...SEX. Let's see...
ARGUMENT. BREAK UP. MAKE UP. SEX ... let's see, then ...
ARGUMENT. ARGUMENT. ARGUMENT. SEX.

KEVIN No, ARGUMENT. ARGUMENT. SEX.

LOUISE No, ARGUMENT. ARGUMENT. ARGUMENT. SEX

KEVIN No.

LOUISE Yes. Anyway, MORE SEX. BIG ARGUMENT. FINAL BREAK UP

KEVIN That's right.

They sit down. Nathan and Marissa enter and stand in front of their chairs.

NATHAN Ours is quite boring in comparison really. Ready?

MARISSA Yes.

They both turn over cards and speak.

NATHAN & SEX. SEX. SEX. SEX. SEX. MINOR SQUABBLE. MAKE UP. SEX. SEX.
MARISSA MARRIAGE. SEX. CHILDREN. LOTS AND LOTS MORE SEX. MORE CHILDREN. STABILITY. GENERALLY HAPPY ENDING WITH REGULAR SEX.

They sit.

GLEN Very good. And ..?

Ivan and Janice enter and stand in front of their chairs.

JANICE SEX. ARGUMENT. BREAK UP. MAKE UP. SEX. ARGUMENT. BREAK UP. MAKE UP. SEX. ARGUMENT. FINAL BREAK UP.

They sit down, pause, then get up again.

CHANCE MEETING. MAKE UP. SEX. ARGUMENT. STAY TOGETHER FOR ALWAYS.

They sit down, pause, get up again.

ARGUMENT. BREAK UP. MEANINGLESS SEX. MEANINGLESS SEX. GENERAL UNHAPPINESS and then,

Pause

and then!

Lovepuke

Pause

> Go on, it's your one, not mine.

IVAN [*sighing*] UNTIMELY DEATH DURING MEANINGLESS SEX

Some other cast members struggle to control laughter.

> It's not funny.

He sits down.

The Beginning

They all sit, clear their throats and turn over their cards to reveal their names.

ALL Marissa, this is Nathan

MARISSA Hi Nathan.

ALL Nathan, this is Marissa.

NATHAN Hi Melissa.

MARISSA Marissa.

NATHAN Oh sorry, Marissa. That's a very nice name.

MARISSA So's yours.

NATHAN Thanks.

ALL Janice, have I introduced you to Ivan yet?

JANICE No.

ALL Oh. Janice - Ivan. Ivan - Janice.

IVAN & JANICE Hi.

Pause.

IVAN	So ... how do you know Susan?
JANICE	I went to school with her.
IVAN	Really?
JANICE	Yep. Best friends we were. How do you know her?
IVAN	I work with her.
JANICE	Oh really?
IVAN	Yeah.
JANICE	Is she still as slack as ever?
IVAN	Susan? Yeah, she spends half of her time sleeping in her office.
JANICE	Nothing's changed.
IVAN	No, good old Susan.
JANICE	Crazy as ever.
IVAN	Yeah. [*Looking Janice in the eye*] I like Susan.
JANICE	[*looking Ivan in the eye*] I like her too.
IVAN	[*to audience*] God, she's attractive.
JANICE	[*to audience*] God, he's beautiful.
KEVIN	[*holding out his hand to shake*] Hey, I couldn't help noticing you across the room. Your face looks kind of familiar, do I know you?
LOUISE	I don't think so.
KEVIN	Well I do now. My name is --
ALL	Kevin!
LOUISE	That's lovely.

Lovepuke

KEVIN   And you are?

ALL   Louise.

KEVIN   Louise. Nice name. Mind if I call you Loo?

Pause

LOUISE   Fuck off.

NATHAN   So water reticulation is quite an important line of work in the scheme of things.

MARISSA   I see what you mean. Can I have some more wine?

NATHAN   I'd like that.

He pours her some wine.

MARISSA   Thanks. I'm going to see my sister tomorrow.

NATHAN   You have a sister?

MARISSA   Yes. She works for a law firm.

NATHAN   That must be interesting. My sister is married.

MARISSA   Really? That must be good ...

Pause

JANICE   [*giggling*] and then there was the time Susan wagged school and stayed at home all day, but her parents came home unexpectedly so she ran and hid outside under a tree. Only it was raining, and ...

She starts giggling again.

IVAN   [*giggling*] What, what?

JANICE   Anyway she stayed there until two o'clock when ...

She can't stop laughing.

IVAN   Keep going.

As Janice keeps talking, Ivan turns to the audience and speaks.

JANICE with IVAN When, when [*she controls herself*] we came to visit her, and she yells out, 'psst, psst', and we turn around and say 'what's that', and she says 'it's me, Susan', and we say 'what are you doing?', and she says 'I'm wagging and Mum's got home!' and we say [*she starts giggling again*] 'Susan, it's Labor Day, it's a public holiday!!!'.

IVAN with JANICE God she's attractive. Her eyes, I could stare at them for ages, I could drown in them, and her tongue, it's so moist and supple, I want to lick it, God I'm on heat, she's just so perfect I could eat her. If I could just go over to her and kiss her. Stay calm Ivan, God, I want to take my shirt off and ...

They burst out laughing together

IVAN That could only be Susan. She's so funny.

JANICE I'll say.

KEVIN [*holding out his hand to shake*] Hey, I couldn't help noticing you across the room. Your face looks kind of familiar.

LOUISE Fuck off.

NATHAN So. Do you play any sports?

MARISSA Not really. I can waterski.

NATHAN Oh really? I like water.

Pause - they both drink.

MARISSA Yes, we both, I mean me and my family both go up to Wanaka together and, and waterski.

NATHAN Does your sister go?

MARISSA Yes.

NATHAN It's a wonder she can spare the time away from her legal work.

MARISSA Yeah, she takes her holidays to fit when we go on holiday.

Lovepuke

NATHAN Good for her.

They both drink.

KEVIN [*holding out his hand to shake*] Hey!

LOUISE Fuck off.

IVAN ... and that was the last time I ever saw my Grandmother. We were very close, excuse me - [*He stops and pulls out a* HANKY; *wipes his eyes a little.*] Sorry, I still get emotional over it ... this is so embarrassing, I don't mean to bring the conversation down.

JANICE No, go on.

IVAN Well, anyway, as I was saying, Susan helped me through it all, she stood by me at the funeral, she came and visited me heaps, she bought me flowers, she was there to comfort me whenever I was down - sometimes I would be feeling at my lowest, almost suicidal, and you know what I would do? I would call Susan and we'd talk, and she'd cheer me up, and everything would be all right for another day. Now, of course, I'm mostly over it [*He wipes his eyes*] although you wouldn't know it, look at me - still, I got through it - thanks to Susan.

JANICE [*to the audience*] God, he's not afraid to cry; that's so rare in a man. This guy is something special - he doesn't put up a mask, he's able to speak about his problems, which is so rare in a man, especially one so attactive with his rugged shoulders and that firm chest, and his long flowing hair. I wonder what he uses, it must be really expensive, and his stubble - I really like stubble on a man, he's so vulnerable at the moment, I want to just reach out and hug him and say everything will be all right as long as you're with me, and to feel his face against my breasts.

[*to Ivan*] Susan is pretty wonderful.

IVAN She sure is.

KEVIN [*clearing his throat*] I'm an accountant. I have a good steady income, loads of money, a big house, a nice car, a fifteen page curriculum vitae and I'm good in bed. I also own a spa pool.

LOUISE I like spa pools. They're so hot and steamy.

KEVIN	I'm --
ALL	Kevin!
LOUISE	I'm horny.
KEVIN	Wow!
NATHAN	It's a nice night.
MARISSA	[*shivering*] Yeah...[*Pause.*] Thanks for walking me home.
NATHAN	It was nothing. [*Pause.*] I like walking.
MARISSA	Me too.
NATHAN	Yes. [*Pause - Marissa is shivering*] Are you cold?
MARISSA	Sort of. [*Pause.*] I've got cold hands. [*Pause.*]
NATHAN	I could hold them if you like.
MARISSA	That would be nice.

They hold hands

GLEN	Stop! Before it's too late! Quit while you're behind. Save yourself a whole load of trouble! It's not worth it! You'll fall in love, things'll go wrong and you'll be miserable. Quit now, and you can be a hip happy single like me! [*He notices the audience.*] Oh hi, I didn't introduce myself. I'm Glen. I'm a cynic. A healthy cynic. Every cynic is a healthy cynic I've always said, especially when it comes to the L word. Believe me, I've been there. I've trodden down that path, done my tour, rode that roller-coaster. The thing that people don't realise is that love is not a roller-coaster. Love is a precipice. You Go for a climb, and the view's very nice but you want to see more, so you keep going higher, except you still want more, and the higher you get the higher you want to be, until eventually you get to the top. From which the only way is down. It's quite a steep drop, isn't it? [*to the characters in the play*] You could all save yourselves the trouble if you stop climbing now. But no - don't listen to me. Go on - play the game. Make your move.

Making the Move

NATHAN	Um, Marissa?

Lovepuke

MARISSA   Yes?

NATHAN   Nothing. [*Pause.*] It's just that I was wondering if ... if maybe ...

Pause.

MARISSA   What?

NATHAN   Oh nothing, leave it.

MARISSA   What?

NATHAN   No, it was just a silly thought.

MARISSA   Oh.

Pause.

NATHAN   It's a nice night.

MARISSA   It's a very nice night.

Pause.

NATHAN   Marissa ...

MARISSA   Yes?

NATHAN   You know how we get on so well ...

JANICE   Yep, Susan's a real diamond. [*To audience*] I want to hold him ...

IVAN   Yeah, one of a kind. [*To audience*] I want to sleep with her.

JANICE   If everyone was like Susan the world would be a better place. [*To audience*] I want to kiss him.

IVAN   Susan is the greatest! [*To audience*] I want to sleep with her.

JANICE   Susan is a special person. [*To audience*] I want to have his babies.

IVAN	She's great. [*To audience*] I want to sleep with her.
JANICE	She's the best. [*To audience*] Three children, two girls, and a little boy
IVAN	She's fantastic. [*To audience*] I want to sleep with her.
JANICE	She's the best friend I ever had. [*To audience*] Gwynneth, Clarissa and Simon.
IVAN	Janice.
JANICE	Ivan.
IVAN	I'm tired. I'm going home.
JANICE	I'll come with you.

Opening strains of Days of Our Lives music. All other cast members applaud.

NATHAN	Anyway, we communicate really well.
MARISSA	Yes we do.
NATHAN	And I was thinking ... [*Pause. Suddenly*] Look at that!
MARISSA	What?
NATHAN	Shit.
MARISSA	Nathan!
NATHAN	Nothing.

Pause.

MARISSA	Are you all right Nathan?
NATHAN	Me? I'm fine. Box of roses, me. [*Sudden inspiration*] Your eyes, remind me of roses.
MARISSA	Do they?

Lovepuke

NATHAN Yes, so sweet, delicate, colourful, nice smelling ...

MARISSA Thank you.

NATHAN [*developing confidence*] Think nothing of it. And you know what? They remind me of something I was going to ask you. Marissa?

MARISSA Yes Nathan.

Pause.

NATHAN Have you got the time?

LOUISE So ...

KEVIN Yeah.

LOUISE You wanna fuck?

KEVIN Yeah.

Opening strains of Days of Our Lives music. All other cast members applaud.

MARISSA 11.30

NATHAN Oh.

Nathan starts to squirm. He moves to say something as Marissa wills him on, but he chickens out at the last second. He looks around at everyone else who has completed making their move, moans even more, squirming uncontrollably, he again attempts to say something while Marissa wills him on, but once again he is unable to speak, his whole body starts to seize up, to the point where he holds his breath and can't let it out again - he is openly panicking, but can't actually do anything. Marissa tries her best to induce him to say something but he is rendered incapable. This goes on for at least a minute, with Nathan incapable of doing anything except a series of nasal moans, before finally Marissa lets him off the hook.

MARISSA [*suddenly*] Do you wanna go out with me Nathan?

Nathan finally exhales.

NATHAN   [*out of breath*] Yeah.

Marissa hugs Nathan who is exhausted. Opening strains of Days of Our Lives music. All other cast members applaud.

GLEN   Applaud them if you like. You're applauding their downfall. It's not too late to pull out you know. Ah, why am I bothering, Go ahead, lose your independence. See, that's what it's all about - independence. As soon as you meet someone you become dependent. You lose strength. As for me, I've got all the independence in the world. I do what I like, when I like it. I answer to no-one but ME. I'm spontaneous. If I feel like doing something, don't try to stop me, because I'm a free spirit and no-one cramps my style. Being single is awesome. Case in point: it's a typical Saturday night. What shall I do? 'What do you think Glen?' 'I don't know, you could turn on the radio.' 'Dammit I might, do you mind if I turn it up really loud?' 'You do what you like Glen, you don't have to answer to anyone but me.' 'I will then - thanks.' 'That's okay Glen.'.

He switches on the radio.

ALL   [*singing 'Another Saturday Night and I Ain't Got Nobody'*
Glen switches the radio off.]

GLEN   Or I could switch it off, on a whim. That's the sort of spontaneous guy independence has made me. [*Pause.*] Yep. The range of possibilities are endless. I could read a book, listen to the radio, watch television . . . bake some fudge and pig out . . . [*He sits down; pause.*] God I'm depressed. Great.

Elation
Great

Long pause. Then everyone except for Glen and Hermione launch into hysterical jubilation.

NATHAN   I can't believe it!

JANICE   It's like a dream!

KEVIN   I'm gonna get laid, I'm gonna get laid!

IVAN   If I play my cards right ...

NATHAN   and don't panic ...

KEVIN   Score! Score! Score! Score!

Lovepuke

LOUISE   It was *so* easy.

MARISSA   Boy, that was tough.

LOUISE   I just walk into a bar and I can have anyone I want.

MARISSA   But it's gonna be worth it.

LOUISE   They come to me.

JANICE   It's like a movie.

LOUISE   Like flies.

JANICE   Fred Astaire and Ginger Rogers.

LOUISE   This is such an ego boost.

NATHAN   She likes me, she likes me!

IVAN   I was so smooth.

KEVIN   She obviously liked my body.

MARISSA   He was putty in my hands.

JANICE   I'm irresistible, like Marilyn Monroe.

IVAN   I am adorable.

NATHAN   I must be great.

LOUISE   I am a machine.

MARISSA   I'm amazing!

KEVIN   I've got a hard on.

ALL   God!

IVAN   Wait 'till I tell the lads.

LOUISE	I'll arrive back at my flat conspicuously at seven in the morning...
MARISSA	My sister will be really jealous.
LOUISE	... all my hair mussed up, and tired looking ...
JANICE	I can't wait for people to see us together.
LOUISE	... that way people are bound to ask questions.
NATHAN	Mum's gonna be so proud.
LOUISE	Of course, I'll deny everything.
KEVIN	I'll have to write to Forum magazine.
LOUISE	But they'll know.
ALL	I'm so excited!!!
IVAN	This is the one, I can feel it in my bones.
KEVIN	Who knows - this could be the woman I marry.
MARISSA	This could be the man I spend the rest of my life with...
JANICE	This is love at first sight.
NATHAN	I think she might be the one.
IVAN	Miss Right.
JANICE	Mr Right.
NATHAN	Mrs Nathan Holloway.
MARISSA	Ms Marissa Holloway.
KEVIN	Mr and Mrs Kevin Anderson.
LOUISE	I hope he's good in bed.

Sex No. 1

Everyone settles into a comfortable position sitting in their chairs. Sex is simulated simply by jiggling up and down on the spot and impassively saying 'ooo aaa ooo aaa' repeatedly and mechanically (deadpan). At timed intervals, couples should turn and smile at each other and return to what they were doing. People should go at the rhythm they feel most comfortable with. This will create an orchestra of low key 'ooo aaa's' which continues as people speak. After less than two seconds of cast ooing and aaing Nathan speaks.

    NATHAN   Yes Yes Yes! ! !

He stands and holds a FIRST sign. Marissa stops jiggling. There is a long pause while 'ooing' and 'aaing' chorus continues. Eventually...

    KEVIN   Yes Yes Yes! ! !

He stands and holds a FIRST sign. Short pause with continued 'ooing' and 'aaing', then ...

    LOUISE   Yes Yes Yes! ! !

She stands and holds a SECOND sign. She sits down and joins chorus of 'ooing' and 'aaing' again. Continuous 'ooing' and 'aaing', then ...

    IVAN   Yes Yes Yes! ! !

He stands and holds a FIRST sign.

    LOUISE   Yes Yes Yes! ! !

She stands and holds a THIRD sign, then sits down again and joins chorus. More 'ooing' and 'aaing', then...

    JANICE   Yes Yes Yes! ! !

She stands and holds a SECOND sign.

    LOUISE   Yes Yes Yes! ! !

She stands and holds a FOURTH sign. She sits down and resumes 'ooing' and 'aaing' while other cast members yawn, check their watches and look at her jealously. Eventually Glen interrupts.

GLEN   Enough!

Louise sighs and simultaneously displays her SECOND, THIRD and FOURTH signs. Marissa stands and looks at everyone else, and displays a DID NOT FINISH sign.

Aftermath

JANICE   There's nothing nicer than lying in someone's arms after sex.

LOUISE   God, I hate this bit.

JANICE   You just close your eyes, and drift away...

LOUISE   There's nothing more awkward than that time after sex.

JANICE   It seems like this moment could last forever...

LOUISE   There's no way to get away...

JANICE   ... feeling at one with someone.

LOUISE   Not without offending your partner anyway.

JANICE   There's nothing better than doing nothing with someone.

LOUISE   And if you can't get away, what are you supposed to do?

JANICE   I can see our wedding ...

LOUISE   Game of cards?

JANICE   All my family is there.

LOUISE   Some intelligent conversation perhaps?

JANICE   Mum's wearing a blue floral hat.

LOUISE   Fat chance.

JANICE   It goes nicely with her blue floral dress.

LOUISE   I mean, when you've just finished bonking someone's brains out, what are you supposed to talk about?

NATHAN	Good night.
MARISSA	Good night.
JANICE	And Dad's wearing a tuxedo.
LOUISE	What can you possibly say?
JANICE	Ivan's wearing a cream suit.
LOUISE	Hey, did you catch the news tonight?
JANICE	I'm walking up the aisle now...
LOUISE	What about Croatia, eh?
JANICE	... and everyone's applauding ...
LOUISE	There's nothing you can say that's not corny.
JANICE	... and everyone's so, so happy...
LOUISE	So you say nothing.
JANICE	... because they know our love is greater than any in the Universe
LOUISE	You just lie there.

Nathan snores.

JANICE	Drift away.
LOUISE	Feeling stupid.

Nathan snores.

MARISSA	Nathan . . .
JANICE	Sweet dreams.
LOUISE	Doing nothing.

Nathan snores.

MARISSA	[*shouting*] Nathan!
NATHAN	[*screams, startled*] What, what!
MARISSA	Sorry - didn't mean to scare you.
NATHAN	What is it?
MARISSA	It's just that you were you were ... Just wanted to say hi.
NATHAN	Hi? You woke me up just to say hi?
MARISSA	Mm. Sweet dreams.
GLEN	One of the advantages of being single is always getting a good night's sleep.
NATHAN	There's nothing worse than being woken up in the middle of the night for no reason.
GLEN	No worry about noisy sleepers.
NATHAN	I can never get back to sleep again.
GLEN	Sheet stealers.
NATHAN	I wonder what Marissa's reading ...
GLEN	Pillow dribblers.
NATHAN	*The Cosmopolitan Lovers' Guide?*
GLEN	Tossers and turners.
NATHAN	[*reading*] How To Be A Better Lover?
GLEN	People that hold you too tight ...
NATHAN	[*reading*] The G Spot.
GLEN	... and keep you warm.
NATHAN	The G Spot is an area that provides erotic sensation in women.

Lovepuke

GLEN	Whisper 'I love you' in the middle of the night.
NATHAN	It was first discovered by Ernest Grafenberg in 1944.
GLEN	People who ...
NATHAN	If his finger enters the ...
GLEN	Women who ...
NATHAN	... enters the ...
GLEN	Beautiful women.
NATHAN	... enters the va--
GLEN	... with no clothes on.
NATHAN	This is disgusting!
GLEN	[*walking off*] I need a coffee.
KEVIN	You are so beautiful -
IVAN	God we look beautiful!
KEVIN	to me.
IVAN	And photogenic.
KEVIN	Can't you see?
IVAN	Janice?
JANICE	Mm?
IVAN	[*clicking a CAMERA*] Smile.
KEVIN	You're everything I hoped for.
IVAN	One of just you. [*He clicks again.*]

KEVIN	You're everything I need.
IVAN	One of just me.
KEVIN	You are so beautiful to me.
IVAN	And a silly one. [*He clicks CAMERA.*]
KEVIN	You are so beautiful to me, Louise.
HERMIONE	Sitting on the loo, There's nothing much to do. I think I'll do a poo It makes me think of you.

Fun and Games

NATHAN	We're playing a few phone games. In this game the object is not to phone the other person first. My reason for playing this game is that the last three times in a row I've phoned Marissa, and I think it's her turn.
MARISSA	My reason for playing is that I want to appear independent, as if I have a life.
NATHAN	It is fascinating to observe two experienced campaigners playing the phone game.
MARISSA	But it's even better watching people who are useless at it, such as Nathan and myself. For example, you get moves like this.
MARISSA & NATHAN	I can't stand this.

They pick up the phone at the same time, and dial.

MARISSA & NATHAN	Engaged.

They put the phones down.

MARISSA & NATHAN	Phew!

Lovepuke

JANICE We're playing a round of fun little games we like to play as an excuse for a little sexual contact in front of our friends. The first one is called, 'Are you ticklish'. Ahem. I bet you're ticklish.

IVAN No I'm not.

JANICE Yes you are.

She goes to tickle him - they have a playfight and end up on the floor.

IVAN These are good games to play because it doesn't matter if you win or lose.

Janice stands on his chair and holds a sign FIRST. Ivan holds SECOND. They shake hands.

LOUISE Kevin and I will be playing two separate games at the same time.

KEVIN I will be playing 'Fishing for a Compliment.' I'm playing this to boost my ego, and so she'll tell me she loves me.

LOUISE While I'll be playing 'I'm a bad person', a game in which I give a bad impression of what I'm really like to make sure the relationship stays nice and short. Let's see how the two games go together.

KEVIN My opening tactic in fishing for a compliment is to play myself down. Ahem. I'm out of shape.

LOUISE He has played into my hands beautifully, with an open offer looking for reassurance, I return it with a joke designed to lower his self-esteem and as a foundation block for putting him off.

[*To Kevin*] I'll say you are. [*To audience*] One-nil, to me.

JANICE I like this game. This one is called 'Silly Nickname in Cutesy Voice'. Ahem. [*In a silly voice*] Ivy, Ivy.

IVAN Shut up.

JANICE IVY.

IVAN I'm warning you.

JANICE Ivy Ivy Ivy.

IVAN   Right.

He lunges at her; they have a playfight and end up on the floor. Ivan stands on chair and holds a sign FIRST. Janice holds SECOND. They shake hands.

MARISSA   The tension is mounting in our game.

Nathan starts to squirm uncontrollably, as he did earlier. He can't breathe properly and seems about to explode, when suddenly Marissa dials him. He answers the phone quickly.

NATHAN   Hello!

MARISSA   [*dejected*] Hello.

NATHAN   I win! ! !

MARISSA   I lose.

NATHAN   [*dejected*] But it doesn't really count because I answered the phone in half a ring, and thus appeared desperate.

They stand on chairs; Marissa holds a SECOND, Nathan holds a HOLLOW VICTORY.

IVAN   This is my favourite. It requires preparation. Its called 'Don't do that or you'll get the frozen teaspoon on the belly button. Ahem. Don't ...

JANICE   I will.

IVAN   Don't.

JANICE   I will.

IVAN   You'll get the frozen teaspoon on the belly button ...

Janice throws something at Ivan. He gets a teaspoon and they have a playfight, ending up on the ground. Ivan holds a sign saying FIRST, Janice one saying SECOND.

KEVIN   In this desperate bid for a compliment I present Louise with an open question in which to give a compliment. The person merely needs to respond positively. Using this method, even a nod will bring success. Here goes. Ahem. Do you think I'm handsome?

Lovepuke

LOUISE An easy victory could be gained by simply offering the short answer, however I will go for extra points by throwing in a clever insult. Once again I disguise it as a friendly witty jibe. Ahem. Compared to what?

KEVIN [*dejected*] Oh.

LOUISE A bonus point for that one. Three-nil, and an easy victory to me.

Louise stands on chair and holds a sign saying FIRST, Kevin displays one saying SECOND.

GLEN I'm playing a stupid game called 'Trying to get a date'. I'll be using a phone also. Is Susan there? Hi Susan, this is Glen ... Glen ... We met at the pub ... Saturday, you ... how drunk? ... Oh well, anyway I was wondering ... Uh huh... Uh huh ... Well, I hope your dog gets better ... Yeah, some other time maybe, see ya. Fuck.

Argument No. 1

NATHAN Our topic is 'Why Are You Reading Such Trash?'

JANICE Our topic is 'What Sort of Ego Have You Got?'

KEVIN Our topic is 'Why Are You Cutting Me Down?'

NATHAN What is this trash?

MARISSA What?

KEVIN Why are you cutting me down?

LOUISE What?

IVAN Janice?

JANICE Yeah?

IVAN Happy Anniversary [*He hands her a piece of cardboard with LOCKET written on it.*]

JANICE It's beautiful.

IVAN Open it up.

JANICE	What's this?
NATHAN	The *Cosmopolitan Lovers' Guide*
MARISSA	What's wrong with that?
NATHAN	Really Marissa. I did expect better of you.
KEVIN	Every time I say something nice you put me down.
LOUISE	Bullshit
IVAN	Don't you recognise it?
JANICE	All I see is a photo of a naked man.
IVAN	That isn't any ordinary person, that's me.
NATHAN	I mean, look at these pictures Marissa. Things like that should not be magnified.
KEVIN	You do. You never say anything nice.
LOUISE	You're talking through a hole in your arse.
JANICE	What sort of ego have you got?!
IVAN	It's all right, I've got one of you as well ... Look.
NATHAN	It's disgusting. I'm going to burn it.
MARISSA	You're kidding, right?
LOUISE	I'm just joking around.
IVAN	I thought you had a sense of humour.
NATHAN	I thought you had better taste in literature.
KEVIN	Yeah, well, a joke or two is fine.

Lovepuke

JANICE   But this is going too far!

MARISSA   Fuck your better taste in literature!

Long pause.

IVAN   Look, I'm sorry I did that. I misjudged the situation.

JANICE   Well, I'm sorry you did it too. [*Pause.*] Still, you won't do it again will you.

LOUISE   Okay, from now on I'll try to be nice.

KEVIN   You mean it?

LOUISE   Yes.

MARISSA   I'm sorry I snapped.

NATHAN   You didn't snap.

MARISSA   Well, sorry if I ever do.

IVAN   Truce?

JANICE   Truce.

LOUISE   Sorry.

JANICE   I'm sorry too.

NATHAN   I'm sorrier than you are.

MARISSA   I'm twice as sorry.

IVAN   We're as sorry as each other.

KEVIN   Hey, lets never argue again.

NATHAN, Okay.
JANICE,
IVAN &
MARISSA

They all hug each other.

Sex No. 2

Everyone is 'ooing' and 'aaing' and jiggling as in Sex No.1 throughout the following piece. Nathan reads from a piece of cardboard that says on one side COSMOPOLITAN LOVERS' GUIDE. On the other side it says ERECTION. Throughout the following, Nathan turns it to reveal the ERECTION to the audience, and slowly crumples it as he gets more and more nervous.

NATHAN   Right, The G spot is an area which provides erotic sensation in women.

MARISSA   What are you doing Nathan?

NATHAN   Nothing. If the finger enters the vagina and presses forward at a depth of about four centimetres ...

MARISSA   Nathan?

NATHAN   [*he measures*] four centimetres ...

MARISSA   Nathan ...

NATHAN   Hmmm ... from the vaginal entrance, it is possible to compress the urethra and the neck of the bladder gently against the pubic bone ...

MARISSA   Nathan?

NATHAN   Shhh, I can't concentrate ... compress the urethra and the neck of the bladder pubic ... no ...

MARISSA   Are you all right?

NATHAN   [*losing breath, in a panic*] Quiet! Compress the finger and turn the pubic bladder into, into ... into ...

Nathan accidentally rips his ERECTION. He stops jiggling.

MARISSA   Nathan, what's wrong?

NATHAN   I can't ...

MARISSA   You can't ...

NATHAN   I can't ... It won't ... I just can't okay!

They stand on their seats, both holding DID NOT FINISH signs.

JANICE   I like to fantasise when I'm having sex. I'm dreaming that Ivan and I are sailing around the world together in a small wooden dinghy ...

IVAN   You know, Janice looks a lot like my ex-girlfriend.

JANICE   ... and I'm sitting opposite him, staring into his eyes while he rows.

IVAN   Well, her hair is a different colour, and she's thinner, but her voice is similar

JANICE   And then, this really big wave catches up with us...

IVAN   She was great in bed.

JANICE   ... and we end up washed ashore on a remote desert island.

IVAN   Great blow-jobs.

JANICE   ... except he's taken in too much water and is unconscious - so I give him mouth-to-mouth

IVAN   I like a good blow-job.

JANICE   ... and I revive him, and we both have hypothermia so we huddle together all night ...

IVAN   Is that a bad thing?

JANICE   ... but then a tribe of pygmies try to eat us, so Ivan fights them.

IVAN   You know, with a little imagination I can picture her face on Janice's body.

JANICE   And he is about to kill one of them but he stops, because Ivan's a pacifist.

IVAN   If I close my eyes, it's like I'm sleeping with her.

JANICE And then they build us a throne ...

IVAN Mmmmmm Marissa.

JANICE ... and then they pronounce us King Ivan and Queen

IVAN Marissa!

Janice stops jiggling. Ivan stops also when he realises what has happened.

JANICE Who?

They stand on chairs holding DID NOT FINISH signs.

KEVIN & LOUISE [*louder*] Oo aa oo aa oo aa ...

GLEN Yes Yes Yes!!! What? Oh it's not how it looks. I was just just um ... Okay, it is how it looks. Yes, I masturbate. But hey! It's no big deal. Everyone does. Don't they? They do. You masturbate don't you? You do, don't you? Denying it. Golden Rule Number One - Deny everything. Obviously lying. Well at least I'm brave enough to be honest. I am a wanker. Isn't everyone? Some of you must be?

KEVIN Yes yes yes!

He holds up FIRST.

GLEN Some of you?

LOUISE Yes yes yes!

She holds up SECOND.

GLEN Any of you?

LOUISE Yes yes yes!

She holds up THIRD.

GLEN One of you?

He slumps to the ground

I'm not having a good day.

KEVIN Wow! I made you orgasm three times.

LOUISE Mmm.

KEVIN I must be pretty hot.

LOUISE Credit where credit's due - it was a good performance.

KEVIN I must be pretty special.

LOUISE You were good. It was good.

KEVIN I'm something else.

LOUISE I do admit it's your one redeeming feature.

KEVIN What, this? [*He laughs.*] Yep. I was damned good.

Pause.

LOUISE [*sarcastically*] Well done.

KEVIN Ha, ha. Do you wanna know my secret, Louise?

LOUISE No.

KEVIN It was love that pulled me through Louise.

LOUISE What?

KEVIN Love, Louise, love.

LOUISE Oh.

KEVIN I love you Louise.

LOUISE I'm married.

HERMIONE	There's a rumbling in my rear Something big in there This one could stain my underwear I wish that YOU were here

Argument No. 2

MARISSA	Our topic is 'Why Won't You Talk to Me?'
KEVIN	Our topic is 'What Do You Mean You're Married?'
JANICE	Our topic is 'Who is Marissa?'
MARISSA	Why won't you talk to me?
KEVIN	What do you mean, you're married?
JANICE	Who the fuck is Marissa!
IVAN	Very bad explanation.
LOUISE	Extremely poor explanation.
NATHAN	No explanation whatsoever, just silence.
JANICE	Demand a better explanation.
KEVIN	Whine and whimper a lot.
IVAN	Short answer, make a joke, change the subject.
JANICE	Raise my voice and demand a straight answer.
IVAN	Vehemently deny accusation, walk away.
JANICE	Demand we discuss this.
KEVIN	Raise my voice and repeat initial complaint.
LOUISE	Condescend with comment designed to make you feel small.

Lovepuke

KEVIN	A direct hit, feeling very, very, small.
LOUISE	[*mock sympathy*] Ohhhhhh.
KEVIN	I want to cry.
MARISSA	New tactic, refuse to talk also.
MARISSA & NATHAN	Stony silence.
IVAN	Best form of defense is offence - hit back with low blow.
JANICE	Low blow parried by blocking ears.
IVAN	Say something I'll regret later.
JANICE	Say a lot of nasty things in the heat of the moment.
KEVIN	Repeat myself over and over again.
LOUISE	Not listening.
KEVIN	Whine.
LOUISE	Mock with an insulting facial gesture.
MARISSA & NATHAN	Stony silence continuing, tension building to explosion point.
NATHAN	Explode! Yell, yell, shout, shout!
MARISSA	Yell louder; low blow.
NATHAN	Curse.
MARISSA	Curse back.
NATHAN	Say something horrible about mother!
MARISSA	Act irrationally in the heat of the moment and break a prized possession.

NATHAN	Swear word swear word swear word.	
MARISSA	Fuck you, too.	
KEVIN	Storm out of room in a rage.	
LOUISE	Give the fingers.	
KEVIN	Storm in to say one final thing.	
LOUISE	Fuck you!	
KEVIN	Fuck you too!	
JANICE	Apologise and attempt to return to rational discussion.	
IVAN	Sex?	
JANICE	No - anger at your insensitivity and refusal to discuss a touchy subject.	
IVAN	Smart comment.	
JANICE	Had enough - get in the last word.	
IVAN	The last word.	
JANICE	The last word.	
IVAN	The final word.	
JANICE	Fuck you.	
IVAN	Fuck you too.	
HERMIONE	I push with all my might But the toilet bowl's still white This one won't come without a fight If YOU were here I'd be all right.	

Problem!

GLEN	Another Saturday night and I ain't got nobody...

Lovepuke

NATHAN	Marissa and I just had a huge argument.
MARISSA	I found out why Nathan wasn't talking to me.
NATHAN	I said a lot of stuff I shouldn't have.
MARISSA	He's impotent.
NATHAN	I guess I lost my head.
MARISSA	Which doesn't bother me in itself ...
NATHAN	I'm not angry at Marissa as such ...
MARISSA	... except I think he blames me.
NATHAN	It's just that I feel so embarrassed when I'm with her.
MARISSA	Because I guess I just don't turn him on.
NATHAN	And I resent her for making me feel this way.
MARISSA	It's affecting everything we do.
NATHAN	It's awful.
GLEN	I got no money and I got no date.
JANICE	Ivan and I patched things up. Marissa is just his ex. It doesn't really bother me, after all, he says he's over her now and I believe him.
IVAN	I can't stop thinking about Marissa.
JANICE	The real problem is, I can't help dreaming about Ivan.
IVAN	I just keep on comparing her to Janice.
JANICE	In my daydreams he's so perfect.
IVAN	And it's not fair to compare them because Marissa is so --

JANICE	But in reality Ivan is so --
IVAN	So perfect.
JANICE	So human.
IVAN	God I miss Marissa.
JANICE	Quite frankly, I'd rather dream about Ivan than be with Ivan.
IVAN	Being with Janice is like a substitute for the real thing.
JANICE	Being with Ivan is like an interruption from the real thing.
GLEN	Another Saturday night and I ain't got nobody.
KEVIN	I had a dream ... Yeah, me and Louise were getting down to it - she was moaning and groaning like a chimpanzee, when suddenly her husband bursts through the door...
LOUISE	I'm not really married.
KEVIN	Now obviously I'm pissing my pants at this point, especially when he undoes his belt buckle --
LOUISE	Just said that to scare him off.
KEVIN	And of course I'm shitting the sheets now --
LOUISE	I mean, I thought we had an understanding.
KEVIN	... and then he takes off his belt ...
LOUISE	I thought it was a one night thing.
KEVIN	... and then he takes off his trousers ...
LOUISE	Or a one week thing, anyway.
KEVIN	And his undies too.
LOUISE	One week is about the right time for a relationship.

Lovepuke

KEVIN   And he just stands there.

LOUISE   Sex on Saturday night.

KEVIN   Right in front of me.

LOUISE   Sex on Sunday morning.

KEVIN   Stark naked.

LOUISE   Sex on Monday's lunch break.

KEVIN   Right in front of me.

LOUISE   Something kinky on Tuesday.

KEVIN   And then I ...

LOUISE   Just a quickie on Wednesday.

KEVIN   I ...

LOUISE   A kiss and a cuddle on Thursday.

KEVIN   I ...

LOUISE   Shake hands on Friday.

KEVIN   We ...

LOUISE   Start again on Saturday.

KEVIN   Dreams are funny aren't they?

LOUISE   I mean he should've known the rules.

KEVIN   Funny things dreams are.

LOUISE   He did pick me up at a singles bar.

KEVIN   God knows what made me dream that ...

LOUISE	You don't pick someone up at a singles bar without knowing the rules.	
KEVIN	You'd think I was homosexual.	
LOUISE	No emotional attachment.	
KEVIN	Which I'm not.	
LOUISE	I use you, you use me.	
KEVIN	I'm not a homosexual.	
LOUISE	We use each other.	
KEVIN	I'm an accountant.	
LOUISE	End of story.	

Pause.

KEVIN	Not a homosexual.
GLEN	I'm in an awful ...
ALL	I'm in an awful ...
GLEN	I'm in an awful ...
ALL	Way ...
HERMIONE	Run out of paper, Just my luck. My fingers will get brown with muck. To make it worse I'm halfway stuck YOU couldn't give a flying ...

Sex No. 3

ALL	Oo aa oo aa yes yes yes!!!

All hold up signs: GLEN, FIRST; IVAN, FIRST; JANICE, DID NOT FINISH; KEVIN, FIRST; LOUISE, SECOND; MARISSA & NATHAN, DID NOT PARTICIPATE

Lovepuke

Argument No. 3

ALL   Debate Dispute Squabble Quarrel Fight Fuck You!!!

All hold signs: IVAN, LOUISE & NATHAN, FIRST; JANICE, KEVIN & MARISSA, SECOND.

Sex No. 4

ALL   Oo aa oo aa Yes Yes Yes!!!

All hold up signs: GLEN, FIRST; IVAN, DID NOT PARTICIPATE; JANICE, FIRST; KEVIN, SECOND; LOUISE, FIRST; MARISSA & NATHAN, DID NOT PARTICIPATE.

Argument No. 4

ALL   Grate Rankle Erupt Abuse Condemn Fuck You!!!

All hold signs: JANICE, LOUISE & MARISSA, FIRST; IVAN, KEVIN & NATHAN, SECOND.

Sex No. 5

ALL   Oo aa oo aa Yes Yes Yes!!!

All hold up signs: GLEN, FIRST; IVAN, FIRST; JANICE, DID NOT FINISH; KEVIN, FIRST; LOUISE, SECOND; MARISSA & NATHAN, DID NOT PARTICIPATE.

Argument No.5

ALL   Shout Shriek Scratch Screech Scream Fuck You!!!

All hold signs: JANICE, LOUISE & NATHAN, FIRST; IVAN, KEVIN & MARISSA, SECOND.

Depression

The following speeches will be delivered to different parts of the audience in a 'one-to-one' style. The speeches should be a progression, beginning with those with the longest speeches down to the shortest, each actor coming in about four lines into the previous person's speech.

LOUISE   Someone called me a slut the other day. It was a friend and they were joking, but it's not the sort of comment that makes you feel good, eh? I mean, sure, I like to have sex, I don't see the problem. I'm sick of people looking down at me. Why should I have to justify it anyway? Anyway, it's good for you, isn't it? Keeps you healthy. It's my hobby. You can never get enough - that's what I say? Actually, that's not true. It can get a bit meaningless after a while. I mean, take me and Kevin. We do it as often as possible, but I've got to admit, afterwards I feel like shit, it's sort of meaningless in a way, I mean - don't get me wrong - it's still good, but its like eating the world's most beautiful pavlova on a full stomach, you just don't appreciate it like you should. That's the difference between making love and fucking. I've only made love once. I really thought he was something special, you know? We did a lot of things together and something just clicked, and making love was the next step, and as soon as we'd done it, he said he 'needed some space' but 'he hoped we could still be friends'. Wanker. Took me a while to get over that one. Did the whole routine - losing sleep, making yourself sick, even thought about suicide a few times. See, that's why I don't fall in love anymore. That's why I only fuck - get the same physical buzz, but your mind doesn't go through the same highs and lows, you just remain sort of, empty.

JANICE   I had a dream this morning, it was a more simple dream than usual. Ivan and I were strolling along the beach. We walked along the coastline, and lots of people were around us - a few children were building sandcastles and there were dogs running along the beach dragging their owners behind them and there were seagulls and sunbathers and everything else that goes along with beaches, and we just held hands and walked along. We didn't say anything. We didn't need to and we kept on walking and the beach got longer and longer and soon there were no other people and the sun was going down, but it didn't matter because we were together and that was all that mattered and then I woke up and Ivan was sitting up next to me. He was playing video games. He had a *Game Boy*, and I whispered to him, 'Ivan', and he said to me,'Hang on, I've almost got the high score', and so I waited, and twenty-five minutes later he lay down next to me and looked me in the eyes and said, 'Twenty-five thousand. I got twenty-five thousand', and then he went to sleep, and that's when I realised that scene at the beach would never happen. That scene at the church would never happen. There was no Queen Janice and King Ivan. We were plain old Janice and Ivan. He works at a book store and I work at the law firm. We have fish and chips on Thursdays and we like to read each other's horoscopes and everything isn't perfect. You know, if life was just a dream, I'd be pretty happy, but it's not and I'm not. I'm not happy at all. I feel sick. I feel really sick.

IVAN   I've been thinking a lot about Marissa lately. Well, all the time, actually. I really let someone special slip through, you know? I can't believe I left her. I was so happy, and I left. I just wanted to find out if it could be any better. I know that this sounds weird, but I guess I was looking for the perfect relationship. Sort of, someone who, when you're with them, every moment is amazing. Of course, that person doesn't exist. You know that feeling you get when you meet someone new, where every day is special, every day you're discovering something new and you just wish you could stay awake twenty-four hours a day and then the gloss starts to fade off and everything becomes 'normal'. I don't like normal. I wanted better than normal. That's why I left Marissa, except now I realise normal wasn't so bad. I can't believe I'm doing this to Janice. She doesn't deserve me. I feel really bad when it comes to Janice because I know it's just temporary, so the longer I spend with Janice, the worse I'll hurt her. I'm only in this 'cos I can't handle being alone. I don't wanna hurt Janice but every moment I delay doing anything makes it harder when the break-up does happen. Breaking up is hard to do. I second that. It takes strength, it takes courage. I should tell her now. I should tell her right now - or maybe I should leave it till tomorrow.

KEVIN Hey, have another drink on me. Ah, it's good to be out with mates. Nothing better, eh? Being with your mates is a nice safe environment. Catch the footie the other day? Good game, eh? Of course, we need a new halfback, Johnson played shit didn't he? Yeah. Still, there's nothing better than waking up in the middle of the night to watch the footie. Did you see that movie before it? What was it called? My Own Private Oedipus or something fucking weird eh? Fags eh? Fags. They shouldn't be showing that sort of shit. People don't want to see that sort of shit. I mean, River Phoenix and Keanu Reeves in bed together. I felt sick watching it. I mean, what do they see in each other? Keanu Reeves is ugly, let's face it, and River Phoenix is ... well he's not so bad you know. I guess if I was a woman I might find him attractive 'cos you know, he's got nice eyes and he's not overweight, which is important. Well, I think it would be. I mean, the sort of guy you want to ... see the cricket? Cairnsy - he's a machine - a machine. Yeah, have another beer. No, no. My shout.

GLEN I'm starting to go crazy eh? You can only stand this sort of thing for so long. I've become good at being alone. You get to be a bit of an expert. You harden up. Look at the world with a cold eye. That way, you'll never get hurt and just when you think you're at your strongest, someone comes along and you go back into what I call 'jelly mode'. Jelly mode is where every time you see someone you start to quiver. Jelly isn't very stable material eh? Last time I was in a relationship was wonderful, eh? And when it crashed, it wasn't pretty. I made myself really ill. I'd throw up in the toilet in the middle of the night. At least when I'm single and I'm down, all I do is hyperventilate. Some people treat this whole single thing like a game. I wish I could do that - out on the prowl, looking for action. It's all pretty pathetic really. It's funny, when you're single all you want out of life is a relationship. When you're in a relationship, often all you want is to be single again. I've been on both sides. It's ridiculous. Human beings are difficult creatures to please. When you look at all the pain and suffering in the world and you realise you're in the top ten percent as far as trauma goes, yet more than half of that ten percent are full-on unhappy. Well, it makes you laugh, doesn't it? You've really got to laugh, 'cos if you can't laugh at that, you're stuffed.

NATHAN I'm fucking it up, aren't I? Slowly but surely, I'm fucking it all up, which is so stupid, because I love her so much and I think she used to love me, but I think that's finished. She's given up on me. I can tell. I don't blame her. I'm hopeless in bed. I'm hopeless and that's such a stupid thing, I mean why should it matter? I shouldn't let it affect anything but for some reason it does when you're so embarrassed you can't even look the person you're sleeping with in the eye. Well, it's not the best of all possible worlds, is it? She doesn't want to talk things through any more. Probably because I'm so damned difficult to get anything out of. I guess it's not worth the effort. I'm really scared. I'm scared it's gonna finish soon, and if that happens, well, if that happens ... [*He can't say anything - he shakes his head.*] I love her, you know that? I love her and I just want everything to be better.

MARISSA I haven't been sleeping much lately. I go to bed, and I think far too much. I need a tranquilizer in my head. Oh, it's not too bad. It's just that me and Nathan ... well, we're not communicating, you know. I don't know what's going on in his head. He just isn't the same any more. It's like, you know how coming home to someone you love is, like something you should look forward to? Well, at the moment, it's something I dread. I'm just getting tired of everything. Tired of him, tired of life, tired of... He won't even sleep with me anymore. What have I done wrong? Am I such a bad person? When you watch someone who adored you so much, slowly get to the point where they dread seeing you, you just, well, put it this way, it's not good for self-esteem. When things go wrong, you become a real martyr, eh? 'Oh woe is me', 'Why is everyone so mean to me?' 'Why is life so cruel?' Everything I think is a cliche. I don't know, I just ... don't ...

She shakes her head.

Resolution?

HERMIONE I've got the constipation blues
and I've got everything to lose
Yeaahhh.
The constipation blues
and I sit here
alone
with my refuse.

Everyone applauds.

Thanks. In about fifteen minutes there'll be some more poetry. In the meantime, grab yourself a drink.

KEVIN That was great. That was just great. It was so sad and moving and ...

LOUISE Kevin, you're blubbering.

KEVIN Am I? Well, it's only because it was so sad and moving and sad and ...

LOUISE You're drunk, Kevin.

KEVIN Am I? Well maybe I should be. Maybe I should ought to be very drunk, 'cos, you know what?

LOUISE What?

KEVIN I need to go to the toilet. Where is it? Hey! Where's the toilet!

LOUISE Kevin!

KEVIN I wanna do number twos, I got the number twos blues.

LOUISE He's drunk.

KEVIN Louise, I love your ... breeze.

LOUISE Shut up, Kevin.

Pause.

KEVIN What?

LOUISE Look, let's go outside.

IVAN Marissa.

MARISSA Hi, Ivan.

IVAN [to audience] God she looks beautiful.

MARISSA [to audience] The one person I didn't want to run into.

IVAN So aah ... how've you been?

MARISSA Good, this is Nathan.

IVAN Nathan.

NATHAN	Hi.
MARISSA	He's my lover.
IVAN	Good-o. Um, this is Janice. Janice, this is my girlfriend Marissa.
JANICE	Marissa, this is my girlfriend Janice.
IVAN	That's what I said.
JANICE	No.
LOUISE	You're drunk and you're embarrassing me.
KEVIN	I'm not embarrassing anything.
LOUISE	Look Kevin, I'll call you a taxi.
KEVIN	[*singing*] I'm a taxi, I'm a taxi. I'm a--
LOUISE	Shut the fuck up, will ya?

Pause.

KEVIN	It's okay. I'll walk home.
GLEN	I loved your poetry.
HERMIONE	Thanks.
GLEN	It was so sad and, and moving. And honest. I think it was really honest
HERMIONE	Oh yeah. Thanks.
GLEN	I liked the way you juxtaposed two such contrasting images, of love and toilets. How did you think of that?
HERMIONE	Dunno ... just wrote it.
GLEN	Wow.
IVAN	Marissa and I are playing a new game.

MARISSA   This game is called 'Pretending You're Really Happy'.

IVAN   The object in the game is to make the person you've split up with, think you're really happy without them. You do this by coming on to the person you're with, while the other person is looking.

MARISSA   Skilled players do this as subtly as possible. Wait until the other person is on the other side of the room, so it doesn't look like you're putting on a display.

IVAN   And make sure you look in their direction as little as possible, and to make those looks, as if you're looking at something else.

MARISSA   I'll begin. Nathan?

NATHAN   Yeah?

MARISSA   Come here.

She hugs him.

NATHAN   What was that for?

MARISSA   Nothing, I just wanted a hug.

IVAN   [*to audience*] What does she see in him? I don't get it. Janice?

JANICE   What?

IVAN   Give us a kiss.

JANICE   No.

IVAN   Oh.

He looks around. Marissa is kissing Nathan.

IVAN   [*to audience*] Oh Man ... The horrible thing about this game is that it leads you to make a real spectacle of yourself. You start groping people in public, just so the other person will get jealous.

He tries to grope Janice; she stops him.

JANICE   No, Ivan.

IVAN   What's wrong?

JANICE   Look. I'm tired. I'm going home.

IVAN   But ...

JANICE   Don't make a scene, Ivan. I just want to be alone.

She goes. Marissa holds a FIRST sign, Ivan holds a SECOND.

GLEN   Wasn't that poetry great?

LOUISE   It was okay.

GLEN   It just had so much strength and vitality.

LOUISE   Wasn't really my thing.

GLEN   Oh. I'm Glen.

LOUISE   Louise.

GLEN   Louise, that's a really nice --

LOUISE   - name, yes, I know, and I'm not in the mood, so don't take this the wrong way, but kindly fuck off.

NATHAN   What brought all this on?

MARISSA   I don't know. Must've been the poetry.

NATHAN   Did you like that?

MARISSA   Yeah, I thought it was beautiful.

NATHAN   It was gross.

MARISSA   No it wasn't. I thought it was a turn-on.

NATHAN   A turn-on?

Lovepuke

MARISSA Nathan?

NATHAN What?

MARISSA I've never been to the Men's Loos before.

NATHAN Oh, yeah.

MARISSA What do they look like?

NATHAN You're kidding.

MARISSA Show me, Nathan.

NATHAN Hey, I'm drunk, but not that drunk.

MARISSA Oh please, Nathan, for once in your life, do something wild and impetuous.

NATHAN What's wild and impetuous about going to the toilet?

MARISSA [*breaking out of the hug*] See, you never do anything I want.

Pause.

NATHAN I'm gonna regret this. [*Leading her out.*] Come on.

KEVIN I managed to sober up a little on the way home, but I was still pretty drunk. I passed by a little gay cafe off the main street. I just went for a look you know, to see what gay people look like and stuff, you know, just curiosity, nothing queer or anything. Anyway, I looked through the window, and I saw a friend of mine, Simon from work, in there by himself. Naturally, I'm no snob, so I went in and said, hello, you know, and sat down and had a drink with him. Yeah ... We talked about all sorts of things - the rugby, the cricket, and that, and it was nice. It was really nice. Anyway, we both got the munchies and Simon said, why don't we go to a late-night restaurant, and I said sure, I mean, why not? No harm in going to a restaurant with a mate, right?

NATHAN Well, here it is.

Other actors form a line with backs to audience - as if at a urinal.

MARISSA Guided tour, please.

NATHAN   Okay. This is a basin - pretty functional stuff really. Soap, hot and cold water ... and this is the urinal, complete with toilet soap, and strangers pissing next to each other ...

MARISSA   How embarrassing it must be.

NATHAN   Very embarrassing.

KEVIN   So there we were, in the restaurant together ... candlelight ... nice music ... and we kept talking ... and Simon was telling me about his latest audit, and I started staring into his eyes ... couldn't help it ... it just felt right ... and then he stopped talking and we just looked at each other, and it wasn't that strange, it just felt sort of, well normal, and nice ... really nice ... and then something not so nice happened. [*Two cast members start waving*] They were friends of Simon's; he introduced us, 'yeah, pleased to meet you ... my name? oh, um ... Kevin, yeah' ... and that was okay. Except then [*rest of the cast begin waving.*] Oh, that's my Aunt Dorothy and all her friends from work. [*He waves back.*] Ow, my teeth, ow, ow. Look Simon, I'm sorry, I've gotta go, toothache ... yeah it is a pity ... yeah ... sure I might see you at work sure ... [*He jumps up.*] Taxi! Taxi! I got the taxi straight home. I really needed to sleep with Louise. Yeah, it was really important we fuck tonight. I just wanted to ...

LOUISE & IVAN   Oo aa oo aa oo aa

KEVIN   Louise!

Ivan keeps 'ooing' and 'aaing' in the background.

LOUISE   Hi, Kevin ... Um, this is Ivan.

Ivan holds his hand out to shake.

IVAN   Oh, sorry.

Kevin runs away.

NATHAN   This is a cubicle.

MARISSA   Let's go in.

NATHAN   Yes, this is inside a male cubicle, once again quite func-- yes, that's the lock, and you'll find that it'll now read ENGAGED on the other side, um, note the

Lovepuke

MARISSA	graffiti on the ...
MARISSA	Oo aa oo aa
NATHAN	On the, Marissa?
MARISSA	Shut up, Nathan.
NATHAN	Oh God.
MARISSA & NATHAN	Oo aa oo aa oo aa

The sound continues in the background.

IVAN	That was a bit embarrassing. It was pretty good though. Just a one-off, you know. Louise and I made sure we both knew the situation. We were both using each other, and that was cool ... She's nothing like Marissa. Eh? I don't know where this leaves me and Janice. Janice? Janice? Jan--

He finds a note.

	Dear Ivan...
JANICE	I'm having another day-dream. I'm in a coma and the doctors all say I'm going to die ...
IVAN	I don't know how to write this ...
JANICE	... and everyone gathers round, and someone holds my hand, and one by one each of them says an epitaph for me.
IVAN	... but when you read this letter I'll be in another country.
JANICE	And there's even a message from the Queen, saying how sorry she is.
IVAN	It's not that I don't like you ...
JANICE	And then finally it's Ivan's turn.
IVAN	I do like you.

JANICE	Except he can't even speak because he's so overcome with grief.
IVAN	I like you a lot.
JANICE	His eyes are bloodshot because he's been crying so much for the last six months.
IVAN	But I think we need some time alone.
JANICE	And all he can do is stammer, 'I love you, Janice'.
IVAN	I don't know when I'll be back.
JANICE	And everyone looks at the two of us ...
IVAN	I might never be back.
JANICE	... and everyone cries for us.
IVAN	I hope you're not mad at me.
JANICE	Because they know that he loves me more than any man has ever loved any woman.
IVAN	Hope you have a good Christmas.
JANICE	Which makes me pretty special.
IVAN	Love, Ivan.
JANICE	And then he hops into my hospital bed with me ...
IVAN	Kiss.
JANICE	... and the shock makes him lapse into a coma also ...
IVAN	Kiss.
JANICE	... and we lie unconsciously in each other's arms ...
IVAN	Kiss.

JANICE   ... for the rest of eternity.

Pause.

JANICE   And then I wake up.

IVAN   Bummer.

JANICE   And I'm not in hospital after all.

IVAN   Isn't Louise great?

JANICE   I'm in a motel a few streets down from where Ivan and I used to live.

IVAN   I mean, she doesn't want a real commitment, but ...

JANICE   And I've got five weeks holidays.

IVAN   You never know eh?

JANICE   So I can go back to sleep.

IVAN   I'm a good catch.

JANICE   And dream it all over again.

IVAN   She'll come round.

NATHAN & MARISSA   Oo aa oo aa oo aa Yes . . . Yes . . . Yes!!!

They stand on their seats and hold up a sign saying FIRST EQUAL. Days Of Our Lives music, and everyone shakes hands with them. Nathan and Marissa thank the others. After the euphoria has died down:

NATHAN   I love you.

MARISSA   I love you.

NATHAN   I love you.

MARISSA	I love you.
NATHAN	I love you.
MARISSA	I love you.
NATHAN	I love you.
MARISSA	I love you.
NATHAN	I love you.
MARISSA	I love you.
NATHAN	I love you.
MARISSA	I love you.
NATHAN	I love you.
MARISSA	I love you.
NATHAN	I love you.
MARISSA	I love you.

Hermione throws up. Pause.

| GLEN | Are you all right? |

| HERMIONE | Yeah. [*Pause.*] Too much to drink. |

Pause.

| GLEN | Come back to bed. |

Everyone looks at Glen.

What? What? All right, you knew this was going to happen, didn't you? Oh yes, you knew, you're so clever! Well, let me tell you something. This hasn't changed me one little bit, I'm as cynical as ever, okay? It's just that when you meet someone as creative, and wonderful and perfect as Hermione, it's only

Lovepuke

rational to go a bit gushy and want to spend all your time with them and dream about spending the rest of our lives in a log cabin ...

He clears his throat.

Anyway, that's about the end. Everything seems to be nicely resolved into a tight little package. As you can see, Marissa and Nathan are happy, Janice is alone at last, for a while anyway, Louise and Ivan have got it on, and Kevin has completely failed to address his homosexuality and will try to fool himself for the rest of his life. As for Hermione and I, we get married in about five years our time, four minutes your time, have a relatively happy life together, admittedly there're a number of rough years, particularly when she gives up performing to have children and is frustrated and we only stay together for the children but all in all once we learn not to expect too much out of life we start to settle down again and live relatively happily. So um, that I guess is the end.

The End

JANICE   Hang on?

GLEN   What?

JANICE   It's not quite the end.

GLEN   What do you mean?

JANICE   Ours drags on a bit.

KEVIN   Same here.

Glen sighs.

The Bit After the End (Reprise)

GLEN   This'd better be quick. Well?

All speak at the same time.

KEVIN & LOUISE   SEX, ARGUMENT, ARGUMENT, MAKE UP, SEX, ARGUMENT, ARGUMENT, ARGUMENT, BREAK UP, MAKE UP, SEX, ARGUMENT, ARGUMENT, ARGUMENT, SEX, MORE SEX, BIG ARGUMENT, FINAL BREAK UP

NATHAN & MARISSA	SEX, SEX, SEX, SEX, SEX, MINOR SQUABBLE, MAKE UP, SEX, SEX, MARRIAGE, SEX, CHILDREN, LOTS AND LOTS MORE SEX, MORE CHILDREN, STABILITY, GENERALLY HAPPY ENDING WITH REGULAR SEX
IVAN & JANICE	SEX, ARGUMENT, BREAK UP, MAKE UP, SEX, ARGUMENT, BREAK UP, MAKE UP, SEX, ARGUMENT, FINAL BREAK UP, CHANCE MEETING, MAKE UP, SEX, ARGUMENT, STAY TOGETHER FOR ALWAYS, ARGUMENT, BREAK UP, MEANINGLESS SEX, MEANINGLESS SEX, GENERAL UNHAPPINESS, and then ...
IVAN	UNTIMELY DEATH DURING MEANINGLESS SEX

Some other cast members struggle to control their laughter.

        It's not funny.

HERMIONE   Sneezing
snotting
salivating.
hit me with your slippery spittle
mucus dribbling from your nasal nozzle
glistening green or rhubarb red
achoo god bless this sneezy slime
what goes out goes quickly.
sniff it pick it roll it flick it
every day in every way
enjoy your own secretions.

ALL   Wise men say.
Only fools rush in
But I can't help falling in love with you.

HERMIONE   Spewing
Vomiting
Barfing
Retching
open all sluices
'cos here come the gastric juices
gut-wrenching exclamations of grisly gunge
go back to where you came from
you vile vesicles of grommet vomit
I'll rid you with this thunder chunder
for what goes down must come up again

Lovepuke

and now it's over it feels better
so enjoy that last secretion.

ALL Stop in the name of love
Before you break my heart
Stop in the name of love
Before you tear it apart
Think it over.

HERMIONE And now here comes the fun one.
Undisputed champion of exultant excrement
feel that rush
no need to wait
let it out
ejaculate
discharge your way to a happy day
let's mix our mush
let's smudge our spunk
those trickling surges of heaven-sent gunk
what goes up will eventually come down so enjoy it while it lasts
every minute of every day
enjoy your own secretions.

ALL Love is in the air
Everywhere I look around
Love is in the air
Every sight and every sound
But I don't know if I feel foolish
Don't know if I feel fine
But it's something that I must believe in
and it's there when I look in your eyes.

HERMIONE Sweating and snotting and snorting and spewing
dribbling and foaming and farting and pooing
pissing and sneezing and burping and chundering
these are my favourite bodily functions
each one accompanied with cerebral malfunctions
love conquers all
including my better senses
love sweat love shit
I love your every bit
new love
true love
snot love

                    screw love
                    let's love
                    lovey dove
                    must love
                    spew love
                    what love
                    our love
                    your love
                    and my love
                    puke love
                    puke love
                    love puke
                    love.

GLEN   Hermione.

HERMIONE   Yes?

Obligatory Happy Ending

GLEN   Will you marry me?

HERMIONE   Yes.

Days of Our Lives music. Everyone showers them with confetti. Cardboard with CONFETTI written on it is ripped into bits and Hermione throws a sign saying BOUQUET into the audience.

THE END.

CURRENCY PRESS TEENAGE DRAMA

There are thirteen titles now published in the series and a complete list can be obtained from Currency Press. Recent titles include:

TWO WEEKS WITH THE QUEEN The Play by Mary Morris adapted from Morris Gleitzman's novel.

Colin is on a mission to speak with the Queen about his brother Luke who has cancer. His hilarious attempts to bypass Buckingham Palace protocol, the exceptional people he meets, and the tragedy that allows him to face his own grief creates a powerful and poignant drama.

SPACE DEMONS The Play by Richard Tulloch adapted from Gillian Rubinstein's novel.

Andrew and his friends try to solve a computer game while coping with real problems in their lives.

BEHIND THE BEAT by Darrelyn Gunzburg.

Commissioned by the multicultural Youth Theatre in Adelaide, the play addresses teenage drinking and the issue of responsibility among friends who are involved with a rock band.

CURRENCY PRESS P.O. Box 452, Paddington, NSW 2021 Tel. (02) 332 1300 Fax. (02) 332 3848